teach yourself®

instant german

elisabeth smith

For over 60 years, more than 40 million people have learnt over 750 subjects the **teach yourself** way, with impressive results.

be where you want to be
with **teach yourself**

For UK order enquiries: please contact Bookpoint Ltd, 130 Milton Park, Abingdon, Oxon OX14 4SB. Telephone: +44 (0) 1235 827720. Fax: +44 (0) 1235 400454. Lines are open 09.00–18.00, Monday to Saturday, with a 24-hour message answering service. Details about our titles and how to order are available at www.teachyourself.co.uk.

For USA order enquiries: please contact McGraw-Hill Customer Services, PO Box 545, Blacklick, OH 43004-0545, USA. Telephone: 1-800-722-4726. Fax: 1-614-755-5645.

For Canada order enquiries: please contact McGraw-Hill Ryerson Ltd, 300 Water St, Whitby, Ontario L1N 9B6, Canada. Telephone: 905 430 5000. Fax: 905 430 5020.

Long renowned as the authoritative source for self-guided learning – with more than 30 million copies sold worldwide – the *Teach Yourself* series includes over 300 titles in the fields of languages, crafts, hobbies, business, computing and education.

British Library Cataloguing in Publication Data: a catalogue entry for this title is available from The British Library.

Library of Congress Catalog Card Number: on file.

First published in UK 1998 by Hodder Headline Ltd, 338 Euston Road, London NW1 3BH.

First published in US 1998 by Contemporary Books, a division of the McGraw Hill Companies, 1 Prudential Plaza, 130 East Randolph Street, Chicago, Illinois 60601 USA.

This edition published 2003.

Typeset by Transet Limited, Coventry, England.
Printed in Great Britain for Hodder & Stoughton Educational, a division of Hodder Headline Ltd, 338 Euston Road, London NW1 3BH, by Cox & Wyman Ltd, Reading, Berkshire.

Hodder Headline's policy is to use papers that are natural, renewable and recyclable products and made from wood grown in sustainable forests. The logging and manufacturing processes are expected to conform to the environmental regulations of the country of origin.

Impression number	10 9 8 7 6 5 4 3
Year	2009 2008 2007 2006 2005 2004

contents

read this first

If, like me, you usually skip introductions, don't! Read on! You need to know how **Instant German** works and why.

When I decided to write the **Instant** series I first called it *Barebones*, because that's what you want: *no frills, no fuss, just the bare bones and go!* So in **Instant German** you'll find:

- Only 358 words to say everything, well ... nearly everything.
- No ghastly grammar – just a few useful tips.
- No time wasters such as 'the pen of my aunt...'
- No phrase book phrases for bungee jumping from the Lorelei.
- No need to be perfect. Mistakes won't spoil your success.

I've put some 30 years of teaching experience into this course. I know how people learn. I also know how long they are motivated by a new project (a few weeks) and how little time they can spare to study each day (½ hour). That's why you'll complete **Instant German** in six weeks and get away with 35 minutes a day.

Of course there is some learning to do, but I have tried to make it as much fun as possible, even the boring bits. You'll meet Tom and Kate Walker on holiday in Germany. They do the kind of things you need to know about: shopping, eating out and getting about. As you will note Tom and Kate speak **Instant German** all the time, even to each other. What paragons of virtue!

To get the most out of this course, there are only two things you really should do:

- Follow the **Day-by-day guide** as suggested. Please don't skip bits and short-change your success. Everything is there for a reason.
- If you are a complete beginner, buy the recording that accompanies this book. It will help you to speak faster and with confidence.

When you have filled in your **Certificate** at the end of the book and can speak **Instant German**, I would like to hear from you. You can write to me care of Hodder & Stoughton Educational.

how this book works

Instant German has been structured for your rapid success. This is how it works:

Day-by-day guide Stick to it. If you miss a day, add one.

Dialogues Follow Tom and Kate through Germany. The English of Weeks 1–3 is in 'German-speak' to get you tuned in.

New words Don't fight them, don't skip them – learn them! The flash cards will help you.

Good news grammar After you read it you can forget half and still succeed! That's why it's good news.

Flash words and flash sentences Read about these building blocks in the flash card section on page 80. Then use them!

Learn by heart Obligatory! Memorizing puts you on the fast track to speaking in full sentences.

Let's speak German *You* will be doing the talking – in German.

Spot the keys Listen to rapid German and make sense of it.

Say it simply Learn how to use plain, **Instant German** to say what you want to say. Don't be shy!

Test your progress Mark your own test and be amazed by the result.

Answers This is where you'll find the answers to the exercises.

▶ This icon asks you to switch on the recording.

Pronunciation If you don't know about it and don't have the recording go straight to page 15. You need to know about pronunciation before you can start Week 1.

Progress chart Enter your score each week and monitor your progress. Are you going for *very good* or *outstanding*?

Certificate It's on the last page. In six weeks it will have your name on it!

Since **Instant German** was first published the euro has become Germany's official currency. Occasionally – as in this book and the recording that goes with it – you will still hear people using (Deutsch)marks.

At the end of each week record your test score on the progress chart below.

At the end of the course throw out your worst result – anybody can have a bad week – and add up your *five* best weekly scores. Divide the total by five to get your average score and overall course result.

Write your result – *outstanding*, *excellent*, *very good* or *good* – on your **Certificate** at the end of the book. If you scored more than 80% enlarge it and frame it!

Progress chart

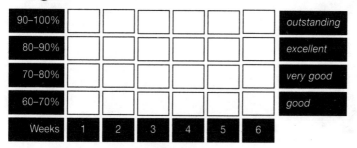

90–100%							*outstanding*
80–90%							*excellent*
70–80%							*very good*
60–70%							*good*
Weeks	1	2	3	4	5	6	

Total of five best weeks =

divided by five =

Your final result ______ %

01 week one

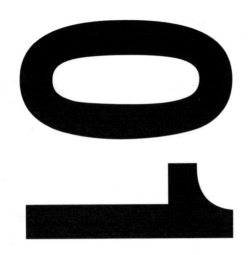

Study for 35 minutes – or a little longer if you can!

Day zero

- Open the book and read **Read this first.**
- Now read **How this book works.**

Day one

- Read **In the aeroplane.**
- Listen to/Read **Im Flugzeug.**
- Listen to/Read the **New words**, then learn some of them.

Day two

- Repeat **Im Flugzeug** and the **New words.**
- Listen to/Read **Pronunciation.**
- Learn more **New words.**
- Use the **Flash words** to help you.

Day three

- Learn all the **New words** until you know them well.
- Read and learn the **Good news grammar.**

Day four

- Cut out and learn the ten **Flash sentences.**
- Listen to/Read **Learn by heart.**

Day five

- Listen to/Read **Let's speak German.**
- Revise! Tomorrow you'll be testing your progress.

Day six

- Translate **Test your progress.**

Day seven is your day off!

In the aeroplane

Tom and Kate Walker are on their way to Germany. They are boarding flight QG 901 to Stuttgart via Frankfurt and squeeze past Klaus Becker, who is sitting in their row.

Tom	Excuse me, we have seat 9a and 9b.
Klaus	Oh, yes, a moment please.
Tom	Hello. We are Tom and Kate Walker.
Klaus	Good day. My name is Becker.
Tom	Boris Becker?
Klaus	No, unfortunately not. I am Klaus Becker.
Tom	We are flying to Stuttgart. You also?
Klaus	No, I am flying to Frankfurt. But I am from Cologne.
Tom	I was in the May in Cologne. The town is very beautiful. I was for my firm in Cologne.
Klaus	What do you do?
Tom	Computers. I work at Unilever.
Klaus	And you, Mrs Walker? What do you do? Where do you work?
Kate	I was in a travel agency. I work now at Rover. The job is better.
Klaus	Are you from London?
Kate	No, we are from Manchester. We were three years in London and a year in New York. We are now in Birmingham.
Klaus	I was at Shell. I am now at the Deutsche Bank.
Tom	How is your job at the bank? Good?
Klaus	The job is boring. But there is more money. I have a big house, a Mercedes, a wife and four children. My wife is from America. She has parents in Los Angeles and a girlfriend in Florida and telephones always. That costs a lot of money.
Kate	We have now holiday. You, too?
Klaus	No, unfortunately not. I have in the September holiday. We are flying to Mallorca – but without the children. We have there a house – without telephone!

Im Flugzeug

Tom and Kate Walker are on their way to Germany. They are boarding flight QG 901 to Stuttgart via Frankfurt and squeeze past Klaus Becker.

Tom Entschuldigen Sie, wir haben Platz neun a und neun b.

Klaus O ja, einen Moment bitte.

Tom Guten Tag. Wir sind Tom und Kate Walker.

Klaus Guten Tag. Mein Name ist Becker.

Tom Boris Becker?

Klaus Nein, leider nicht. Ich bin Klaus Becker.

Tom Wir fliegen nach Stuttgart. Sie auch?

Klaus Nein, ich fliege nach Frankfurt. Aber ich bin aus Köln.

Tom Ich war im Mai in Köln. Die Stadt ist sehr schön. Ich war für meine Firma in Köln.

Klaus Was machen Sie?

Tom Computer. Ich arbeite bei Unilever.

Klaus Und Sie, Frau Walker? Was machen Sie? Wo arbeiten Sie?

Kate Ich war in einem Reisebüro. Ich arbeite jetzt bei Rover. Der Job ist besser.

Klaus Sind Sie aus London?

Kate Nein, wir sind aus Manchester. Wir waren drei Jahre in London und ein Jahr in New York. Wir sind jetzt in Birmingham.

Klaus Ich war bei Shell. Ich bin jetzt bei der Deutschen Bank.

Tom Wie ist Ihr Job bei der Bank? Gut?

Klaus Der Job ist langweilig. Aber es gibt mehr Geld. Ich habe ein grosses Haus, einen Mercedes, eine Frau und vier Kinder. Meine Frau ist aus Amerika. Sie hat Eltern in Los Angeles und eine Freundin in Florida und telefoniert immer. Das kostet viel Geld.

Kate Wir haben jetzt Urlaub. Sie auch?

Klaus Nein, leider nicht. Ich habe im September Urlaub. Wir fliegen nach Mallorca – aber ohne die Kinder. Wir haben da ein Haus – ohne Telefon!

New words

Learning vocabulary is always tedious. Say these words OUT LOUD and don't worry because tomorrow you'll have **flash cards** to play with!

in / im *in / in the*
Flugzeug *aeroplane*
entschuldigen Sie *excuse me*
wir *we*
haben, habe / hat *have / has*
Platz *place, seat*
a ... b (pronounced *ah ... bay*)
und *and*
ja *yes*
ein, eine, einem, einen *a*
Moment *moment*
bitte *please*
guten Tag *hello, good day*
sind *are*
mein, meine *my*
Name *name*
ist *is*
nein *no*
leider *unfortunately*
nicht *not*
ich *I*
bin *am*
fliegen / fliege *fly / are flying, am flying*
nach *to, after*
Sie *you* (polite)
auch *also*
aber *but*
aus *from, out of*
war / waren *was / were*
Mai *May*
der, die, das, dem, den *the*
Stadt *town, city*
sehr *very*
schön *beautiful, lovely, handsome*
für *for*
Firma *firm, company, office*
was *what*
machen / mache *make, do, are doing / am doing*
arbeiten / arbeite *work, are working / am working*
bei *at*
Frau *Mrs, woman, wife*
wo *where*
Reisebüro *travel office, travel agency*
jetzt *now*
besser *better*
drei *three*
Jahr, Jahre *year, years*
wie *how*
Ihr, Ihre, Ihrem, Ihren *your*
gut *good*
langweilig *boring*
es gibt *there is, there are* (lit. *it gives*)
mehr *more*
Geld *money*
gross, grosse, grosses *big*
Haus *house*
vier *four*
Kinder *children*
sie *she*
Eltern *parents*

Freundin *girlfriend*
telefonieren / telefoniert *telephone / telephones*
immer *always*
das (by itself) *that*
das kostet *that costs*
viel *much, a lot of*
Urlaub *holidays*
ohne *without*
da *there*
Telefon *telephone*

TOTAL NEW WORDS: 70
...only 289 words to go!

Some easy extras

These are all very similar to the English!

die Monate (the months)

Januar, Februar, März, April, Mai, Juni, Juli, August, September, Oktober, November, Dezember

Zahlen (numbers)

null	eins	zwei	drei	vier	fünf	sechs	sieben	acht	neun	zehn
0	1	2	3	4	5	6	7	8	9	10

More greetings

hallo *hello*
guten Morgen *good morning*
guten Abend *good evening*
gute Nacht *good night*
auf Wiedersehen *goodbye*

Pronunciation

If German pronunciation is new to you, please buy the recording. But if you are good at languages, or would like a refresher, here are the rules:

First the vowels

The English word in brackets gives you an example of the sound. Say the sound OUT LOUD and then say the German examples OUT LOUD. They can vary a little, but don't worry – near enough is good enough!

a (*star/cut*) ja, Tag, war, da, Name, haben / das, nach, hatte
e (*yes/name*) der, es, jetzt, dem, Dezember, Oktoberfest
i (*in/feel*) in, ist, bin, Firma, wir
o (*no/pot*) gross, oder, kostet
u (*June/good*) gut, Juni, Juli, und

Now the doubles

ei / ai (*fly*) nein, drei, klein, langweilig, Mai
ie (*field*) Sie, wie, vier, telefoniert, viel, fliegen
au (*house*) Haus, Frau, auch, aus, August

Now the consonants

j (like *y* in *y*es) ja, Juni, Juli
s (like *z* in *z*ero) Sie, sind, September
v (like *f* in *f*eel) viel, vier
w (like *v* in *v*an) was, wo, wie
z (like *ts* in *ts*ar) zwei, Platz, Dezember
sch (like *sh* in *sh*ip) schön, Schiff (*ship*), entschuldigen Sie
ch (like the *ch* in lo*ch*), after **a, o** and **u** nach, noch, Kuchen
ch (like an exaggerated **h** in *H*ugh), after **e, i** and **ö**: ich, schlecht, möchten

The famous *Umlauts*

ä (*care*) März, Mädchen
ö (*curve*) schön, zwölf, können (*can*)
ü This is a tricky one with no English equivalent. Try the way a Scotsman would say *noo* in *och aye the noo*.
Then say: fünf, Frühstück, Reisebüro

And some more doubles

ee (*say*) Tee, Kaffee
eu / äu (*toy*) teuer, neu, neun, Verkäufer (*sales assistant*)

Everything is pronounced in German: **Name** is not 'Nam' but **'Na-me'**. Are you tearing your hair out? Why not treat yourself to the recording?

Goods news grammar

This is the Good news part of each lesson. Remember that promise: no ghastly grammar? Every week I explain just a few things and talk you through the differences between English and German. This will help you to speak German **Instantly.**

1 *Der, die, das*

der, die, das, den, dem	→	all mean *the*
ein, eine, einen, einem	→	all mean *a*

Example der Platz, die Firma, das Geld, ein Haus, eine Frau.

So how do you know when to use which? Here's the first of the good news: In **Instant German** there is no need to struggle with what's what. You may muddle up your **der, die, das** and everyone will understand you perfectly!

2 Saying 'you'

Germans usually use **Sie** (with a capital **S**) when talking to each other. This is a formal way of saying *you* and is always used – except to family, best friends and children, who are called **du**. When in Germany stick to **Sie**. It's much easier to use!

3 Doing things – remember to drop an 'n'

When you want to say *I fly*, *I do* or *I have* you drop the **n** from the end of the verb.

Example fliegen becomes **ich fliege**, machen **ich mache**.

4 Asking questions

Easy! You simply reverse the word order.

Example	*You fly...*	**Sie fliegen...**
	Do you fly...?	**Fliegen Sie...?**
	You have...	**Sie haben...**
	Do you have / have you?	**Haben Sie...?**

5 'There is', 'there are'

Use es **gibt** for both of these. You will use this a lot, especially when asking questions:

Example	**Gibt es hier eine Bank?**	*Is there a bank here?*
	Es gibt mehr Geld in Amerika.	*There is more money in America.*

6 Capital letters

All proper names and names of things (nouns) start with a capital letter in German: **Firma, Hans, Name, Geld, Kinder, Urlaub.**

Learn by heart

Don't be tempted to skip this exercise because it reminds you of school ... If you want to **speak,** not stumble, saying a few lines by heart does the trick. Learn **Mein Name ist** ... by heart after you have filled in the gaps with your personal, or any, information.

Example Mein Name ist Amanda Hurley.
Ich bin aus Birmingham.

When you know the seven lines by heart go over them again until you can say them out loud fluently and fairly fast. Can you beat 40 seconds? Excellent!

Mein Name ist ... .

Mein Name ist ... .
Ich bin aus ... .
Ich arbeite für eine grosse Firma.
Wir haben ein schönes Haus, aber es kostet viel Geld.
Ich war im Dezember in ... .
Wir fliegen im Juli nach ... .
Wie war Ihr Urlaub, gut oder langweilig?

Let's speak German

If you have the recording, listen to check the answers to **Let's speak German.**

Here are ten English sentences. Read each sentence and say it in German – OUT LOUD.

1 My name is Walker.
2 Are you from London?
3 Yes, I am from London.
4 I have a girlfriend in Bonn.
5 We are flying to Stuttgart.
6 Do you have a Mercedes?
7 No, unfortunately not.
8 We have a house in Dresden.
9 There is more money in Köln.
10 How was your day, good?

Well, how many did you tick? If you are not happy do it again.

Now here are some questions in German for you to answer in German. For the first five questions answer with **ja** and **ich** and for the last five questions use **nein** and **wir.**

11 Sind Sie aus Manchester?
12 Haben Sie ein Haus in London?
13 Fliegen Sie nach Frankfurt?
14 Arbeiten Sie ohne Computer?
15 Waren Sie für Ihre Firma in Bristol?
16 Fliegen Sie nach Berlin?
17 Haben Sie sechs Kinder?
18 Haben Sie im April Urlaub?
19 Waren Sie ein Jahr in New York?
20 Haben Sie jetzt mehr Geld?

Answers

1 Mein Name ist Walker.
2 Sind Sie aus London?
3 Ja, ich bin aus London.
4 Ich habe eine Freundin in Bonn.
5 Wir fliegen nach Stuttgart.
6 Haben Sie einen Mercedes?
7 Nein, leider nicht.
8 Wir haben ein Haus in Dresden.
9 Es gibt mehr Geld in Köln.
10 Wie war Ihr Tag, gut?
11 Ja, ich bin aus Manchester.
12 Ja, ich habe ein Haus in London.
13 Ja, ich fliege nach Frankfurt.
14 Ja, ich arbeite ohne Computer.
15 Ja, ich war für meine Firma in Bristol.
16 Nein, wir fliegen nicht nach Berlin.
17 Nein, wir haben nicht sechs Kinder.
18 Nein, wir haben nicht im April Urlaub.
19 Nein, wir waren nicht ein Jahr in New York.
20 Nein, wir haben jetzt nicht mehr Geld.

Well, what was your score? If you got 20 ticks you can give yourself three gold stars!

Test your progress

This is your only written exercise. You'll be amazed how easy it is!

Translate the 20 sentences without looking at the previous pages.

1 My name is Peter Smith.
2 Good day, we are Helen and Elke.
3 I am also from Hamburg.
4 I was in Frankfurt in October.
5 My wife and I were in America (for) three years.
6 We always fly to Berlin in June.
7 How was your holiday in England?
8 Excuse me please, what do you do now in London?
9 Are you Mrs Becker from Bonn?
10 The house in Hanover is for my children.
11 One moment please, I have the money.
12 Is there a telephone here? No, unfortunately not.
13 I am in England without my wife.
14 How big is your company?
15 Does a Mercedes cost a lot of money?
16 England is unfortunately not beautiful in February.
17 Udo has a girlfriend in the travel agency.
18 The day in Holland was boring.
19 My job is very good, but (a) holiday is better.
20 My two children have a lot of money.

When you have finished all 20 sentences look up the answers on page 74, and mark your work. Then enter your result on the Progress chart on page 9. If your score is higher than 80% you'll have done very well indeed!

02 week two

Thirty-five minutes a day – but a little extra will step up your progress!

Day one

- Read **In the Black Forest**.
- Listen to/Read **Im Schwarzwald.**
- Listen to/Read the **New words.** Learn 20 easy ones.

Day two

- Repeat **Im Schwarzwald** and the **New words**.
- Go over **Pronunciation.**
- Learn the harder **New words**.
- Use the **Flash words** to help you.

Day three

- Learn all the **New words** until you know them well.
- Read and learn the **Good news grammar**.

Day four

- Cut out and learn the ten **Flash sentences**.
- Listen to/Read **Learn by heart**.

Day five

- Listen to/Read **Let's speak German**.
- Go over **Learn by heart**.

Day six

- Translate **Test your progress**.

Day seven is a study-free day!

In the Black Forest

In Stuttgart Tom and Kate hire a car and drive through the Black Forest. They speak to Ilse Wolf of Pension Wolf.

Kate Good day. Do you have a double room for one night and not too expensive?

Ilse Yes, we have a room with bath and shower. But the shower is broken. My husband can that perhaps repair.

Tom Where is the room?

Ilse It is here left. Is it big enough?

Kate The room is a little small and dark, but not bad. How much is it?

Ilse Only 75 Deutschmarks for two, but no credit cards! There is breakfast from eight to half past nine.

Tom Well..., we would like the room. But can we the breakfast at a quarter to eight have? We would like tomorrow at a quarter past eight to Freiburg go.

Kate And I have a question: where can one coffee or tea drink? Where is there here a café?

Ilse There is a café five minutes from here, 30 metres right and then always straight on.

(In the café.)

Waiter What would you like, please?

Kate We would like a cup coffee and a tea with milk.

Waiter Would you like also something to eat? We have apple cake.

Tom Two apple cakes, once with cream and once without, please.

Tom My cake is terrible

Kate But the cream is good.

Tom The table is too small.

Kate But the toilets are very clean

Tom My tea is cold.

Kate But the waiter is handsome.

Tom The bill, please!

Waiter Nineteen Deutschmarks twenty (pfennigs).

Im Schwarzwald

In Stuttgart Tom and Kate hire a car and drive through the Black Forest. They speak to Ilse Wolf of Pension Wolf.

Kate Guten Tag. Haben Sie ein Doppelzimmer für eine Nacht und nicht zu teuer?

Ilse Ja, wir haben ein Zimmer mit Bad und Dusche. Aber die Dusche ist kaputt. Mein Mann kann das vielleicht reparieren.

Tom Wo ist das Zimmer?

Ilse Es ist hier links. Ist es gross genug?

Kate Das Zimmer ist ein bisschen klein und dunkel, aber nicht schlecht. Wieviel kostet es?

Ilse Nur fünfundsiebzig (75) Mark für zwei, aber keine Kreditkarten! Es gibt Frühstück von acht bis halb zehn.

Tom Also... wir möchten das Zimmer. Aber können wir das Frühstück um viertel vor acht haben? Wir möchten morgen um viertel nach acht nach Freiburg fahren.

Kate Und ich habe eine Frage: Wo kann man Kaffee oder Tee trinken? Wo gibt es hier ein Café?

Ilse Es gibt ein Café fünf Minuten von hier, dreissig Meter rechts und dann immer geradeaus.

(Im Café.)

Kellner Was möchten Sie bitte?

Kate Wir möchten eine Tasse Kaffee und einen Tee mit Milch.

Kellner Möchten Sie auch etwas essen? Wir haben Apfelkuchen.

Tom Zwei Apfelkuchen, einmal mit Sahne und einmal ohne, bitte.

Tom Mein Kuchen ist schrecklich.

Kate Aber die Sahne ist gut.

Tom Der Tisch ist zu klein.

Kate Aber die Toiletten sind sehr sauber.

Tom Mein Tee ist kalt.

Kate Aber der Kellner ist schön.

Tom Die Rechnung, bitte!

Kellner Neunzehn Mark zwanzig.

New words

Learning words the traditional way can be rather boring. If you enjoyed working with the **flash cards**, why not make your own for the rest of the words. Always remember to say the words OUT LOUD – it's the fast track to speaking!

Doppelzimmer *double room*
Zimmer *room*
Nacht *night*
zu *too*
teuer *expensive*
mit *with*
Bad *bath*
Dusche *shower*
kaputt *broken*
Mann *man, husband*
kann, können *can*
vielleicht *perhaps*
reparieren *(to) repair*
es *it*
hier *here*
links *left*
genug *enough*
ein bisschen *a little*
klein, kleine, kleines *small*
dunkel *dark*
schlecht *bad*
wieviel *how much / many*
nur *only*
fünfundsiebzig *seventy-five* (five-and-seventy)
Mark (DM) *Deutschmark*
kein, keine *no*
Kreditkarte *credit card*
Frühstück *breakfast*
von *from*
bis *until*
halb *half*
halb zehn *half past NINE*
also... *well...*
möchten *would like*
um *at* (a certain time)
viertel *quarter*
vor *before*
viertel vor *quarter to*
morgen *tomorrow*
viertel nach *quarter past*
fahren *drive / travel / go*
Frage *question*
man *one*
Kaffee *coffee*
oder *or*
Tee *tea*
trinken *drink*
Café *café*
Minuten *minutes*
dreissig *thirty*
Meter *metre*
rechts *right*
dann *then*
geradeaus *straight on*
Kellner *waiter*
Tasse *cup*
Milch *milk*
etwas *some, something*
essen / gegessen *eat / eaten*
Kuchen, Apfelkuchen *cake, apple cake*
einmal *once*
Sahne *cream*
schrecklich *terrible*
Tisch *table*

Toilletten *the toilets*
sauber *clean*
kalt *cold*
Rechnung *bill*
neunzehn, zwanzig *nineteen, twenty*

TOTAL NEW WORDS: 69
...only 219 to go!

Some easy extras

Zahlen (numbers)

11	**elf**
12	**zwölf**
13	**dreizehn**
14	**vierzehn**
15	**fünfzehn**
16	**sechzehn**
17	**siebzehn**
18	**achtzehn**
19	**neunzehn**
20	**zwanzig**
30	**dreissig**
40	**vierzig**
50	**fünfzig**
60	**sechzig**
70	**siebzig**
80	**achtzig**
90	**neunzig**
100	**hundert**
200	**zweihundert**
300	**dreihundert**
700	**siebenhundert**
1,000	**tausend**

Zeit (time)

Uhr	*clock*
um ... Uhr	*at ... o'clock*
um wieviel Uhr?	*at what time?*
eine Minute	*a minute*
eine Stunde	*an hour*
ein Tag	*a day*
eine Woche	*a week*
ein Monat	*a month*
ein Jahr	*a year*

Numbers up to 20 are very similar to the English. After 20 you say the number for the *unit* first: 24: **vierundzwanzig**. 42: **zweiundvierzig**.

Watch out for the time

halb zehn: think of it as *half towards ten* = 9.30
halb vier = *half towards four* = 3.30, **halb eins** = 12.30

Good news grammar

1 Drop the 'n'

Remember to drop the **n** at the end of verbs when you say **ich**: **essen** becomes **ich esse**; **trinken** becomes **ich trinke**. Here's an odd one out: **können** becomes **ich kann**.

2 Splitting verbs

Germans like to keep you in suspense!

When they say: *We would like to eat Apfelstrudel with cream.*

They actually say: *We would like Apfelstrudel with cream ... (to) eat.*

Wir möchten Apfelstrudel mit Sahne ... essen.

So you don't know right to the end what they are going to do to the cake – *buy* it, *bake* it, or perhaps *eat* it!

What happens is that, when there are two verbs in a sentence, such as **möchten** and **essen**, the second one gets shoved to the very end of the sentence. **Können wir ein Zimmer mit Bad ... haben? Ich möchte morgen in meinem Mercedes 600 nach Freiburg ... fahren.** If you forget and say: **Können wir haben ein Zimmer mit Bad?** there may be smiles all round, but everyone will understand you.

Learn by heart

Learn the following seven lines by heart. Try to say them in under 50 seconds and with a bit of drama! Choose one of the following to fill in the gap: meinem Mann; meiner Frau; meinem Freund (*boy / male friend*); meiner Freundin.

Ich habe nicht viel Geld, aber ... .

Ich habe nicht viel Geld, aber ich möchte im Mai eine Woche Urlaub machen. Ich möchte mit ____ nach Frankfurt fliegen. Ich möchte von Frankfurt in einem grossen Mercedes nach Freiburg fahren. Ich möchte im Schwarzwald viel Bier trinken und Kuchen essen. Kann ich das machen? Ja, meine Firma hat ein gutes Reisebüro. Der Flug und eine Woche in der Pension Wolf sind nicht zu teuer. Es kostet nur 700 Mark.

Urlaub machen: *to make/have a holiday*; Flug: *flight*.

Let's speak German

Over to you! I'll give you ten English sentences and you say them in German OUT LOUD! If you don't have the recording, check your answers against those printed below – but cover them so that you can see only one at a time.

1 We would like a double room.
2 It is unfortunately too expensive.
3 At what time is there breakfast?
4 The telephone is broken.
5 We would like to drink something.
6 Do you also have something to eat?
7 Where is the café, left or right?
8 The cup is not clean.
9 Can I please have the bill?
10 I am in London at nine o'clock tomorrow.

Now here are some questions in German. Use **ja** and **wir** for the ones on the left and **nein** and **ich** for those on the right.

11 Haben Sie eine Kreditkarte?
12 Möchten Sie nach Berlin fahren?
13 Haben Sie hier ein Telefon?
14 Möchten Sie um acht Uhr essen?
15 Können Sie morgen arbeiten?
16 Möchten Sie das Zimmer?

Now think up your own answers. Yours might be different from mine but still be correct.

17 Wo gibt es ein Café hier?
18 Um wieviel Uhr möchten Sie essen?

Answers

1 Wir möchten ein Doppelzimmer.
2 Es ist leider zu teuer.
3 Um wieviel Uhr gibt es Frühstück?
4 Das Telefon ist kaputt.
5 Wir möchten etwas trinken.
6 Haben Sie auch etwas zu essen?
7 Wo ist das Café, links oder rechts?
8 Die Tasse ist nicht sauber.
9 Kann ich bitte die Rechnung haben?
10 Ich bin morgen um neun Uhr in London.
11 Ja, wir haben eine Kreditkarte.
12 Ja, wir möchten nach Berlin fahren.
13 Ja, wir haben hier ein Telefon.
14 Nein, ich möchte nicht um acht Uhr essen.
15 Nein, ich kann nicht morgen arbeiten.
16 Nein, ich möchte das Zimmer nicht.
17 Es gibt ein Café **fünf Minuten** von hier.
18 Wir möchten um **viertel nach sieben essen.**

Well, did you score another 20 out of 20, and collect 3 gold stars?

Test your progress

Translate these sentences into German and write them out.

See what you can remember without looking at the previous pages.

1 I drink a lot of beer.
2 How much is (costs) the breakfast, please?
3 Is there a travel agency here?
4 Do you have a table? In 15 minutes?
5 I would like to drink something.
6 My holiday in Florida was very good.
7 Where is there a good bed and breakfast place?
8 Can I have the bill for the telephone, please?
9 We were in Köln only once.
10 My children are big enough now.
11 At what time are you in the office tomorrow?
12 I am always there from half past seven to a quarter past five.
13 A question please: where are the toilets, straight ahead?
14 We would like to fly to Oslo in January. But it is too cold.
15 Does that cost more money?
16 Where are you tomorrow at half past ten?
17 It is terrible, there is not one job without a computer.
18 Can we eat here now, and do you have seats for six?
19 We have a small house in America, but it was very expensive.
20 Goodbye, we are going to Hamburg now.

Check your answers with the key on page 75 and work out your score. If it is above 70% you have done very well.

Now enter your result on the Progress chart in the front of the book.

03 week three

Study for 35 minutes a day – but there are no penalties for doing more!

Day one

- Read **We are going shopping**.
- Listen to/Read **Wir gehen einkaufen**.
- Read the **New words**, then learn some of them.

Day two

- Repeat the story and the **New words**.
- Learn all the **New words**. Use the **Flash cards**!

Day three

- Test yourself on all the **New words** – boring, boring, but you are over halfway already!
- Learn **Good news grammar**.

Day four

- Cut out and learn ten **Flash sentences**.
- Listen to/Read **Learn by heart**.

Day five

- Listen to/Read **Spot the keys**.
- Listen to/Read **Let's speak German**.

Day six

- Have a quick look at the **New words**, Weeks 1–3.
- You now know 205 words! Well, more or less.
- Translate **Test your progress**.

Day seven: Enjoy your day off!

We are going shopping

Tom and Kate are in Stuttgart. They have rented a holiday apartment for a week. Kate plans some shopping.

Kate Well, we must today do the shopping. We are going with the bus into the centre.

Tom But the weather is bad. It is cold, and there is a lot of sport in the television … Golf at half past twelve …

Kate I am sorry, but we must (go) first to a cash dispenser at the bank and to the post office for stamps … and then to the chemist's and to the dry cleaner's.

Tom Well, no golf … perhaps football at three … Is that all?

Kate No, we must (go) also in a department store and a new suitcase buy, and I must (go) to the supermarket and to the hairdresser's. And I would also like to (go) in a shoe shop.

Tom Oh, good grief! Until when are the shops open?

Kate I believe until six o'clock or eight.

Tom Ah well, also no football … perhaps tennis at half past eight ...

(*Later.*)

Kate I think I have too much bought. 200 g ham, a piece cheese, a half kilo sauerkraut, a kilo potatoes, six Vienna sausages, bread, butter, eggs, sugar, four bottles beer and a bottle wine.

Tom No problem. That is enough for tomorrow. We have yesterday not much eaten. And what is in the big bag? Something for me?

Kate No, yes … Well, I was at Karstadt, at the hairdresser's, and I have in a shop shoes seen, exactly my size. Are they not super? – dark blue with white. The sales assistant was very nice and as handsome as Tom Cruise.

Tom Who is Tom Cruise? And how much cost the shoes?

Kate They were a little expensive. But they cost the same in England … 350 deutschmarks …

Tom What? … That is crazy!

Kate But this T-shirt for golf was very cheap, size 44, only 25 Deutschmarks, wool with cotton, and here is an English newspaper … and is there not now tennis in the television?

Wir gehen einkaufen

Tom and Kate are in Stuttgart. They have rented a holiday apartment for a week. Kate plans some shopping.

Kate Also, wir müssen heute einkaufen. Wir fahren mit dem Bus ins Zentrum.

Tom Aber das Wetter ist schlecht. Es ist kalt, und es gibt viel Sport im Fernsehen ... Golf um halb eins ...

Kate Es tut mir Leid, aber wir müssen zuerst zu einem Geldautomaten bei der Bank und zur Post für Briefmarken ... und dann zur Apotheke und zur Reinigung.

Tom Also kein Golf ... vielleicht Fussball um drei ... Ist das alles?

Kate Nein, wir müssen auch in ein Kaufhaus und einen neuen Koffer kaufen, und ich muss zum Supermarkt und zum Friseur. Und ich möchte auch in ein Schuhgeschäft.

Tom Ach, du meine Güte! Bis wann sind die Geschäfte offen?

Kate Ich glaube bis sechs Uhr, oder acht.

Tom Ach, also auch kein Fussball ... vielleicht Tennis um halb neun ...

(*Später.*)

Kate Ich glaube, ich habe zuviel gekauft: 200 Gramm Schinken, ein Stück Käse, ein halbes Kilo Sauerkraut, ein Kilo Kartoffeln, sechs Wiener, Brot, Butter, Eier, Zucker, vier Flaschen Bier und eine Flasche Wein.

Tom Kein Problem. Das ist genug für morgen. Wir haben gestern nicht viel gegessen. Und was ist in der grossen Tüte? Etwas für mich?

Kate Nein, ja... Also ich war bei Karstadt beim Friseur, und ich habe in einem Geschäft Schuhe gesehen, genau meine Grösse. Sind sie nicht super? – dunkelblau mit weiss. Der Verkäufer war sehr nett und so schön wie Tom Cruise.

Tom Wer ist Tom Cruise? Und wieviel kosten die Schuhe?

Kate Sie waren ein bisschen teuer. Aber sie kosten dasselbe in England ... 350 Mark ...

Tom Was? ... Das ist verrückt!

Kate Aber dieses T-Shirt für Golf war sehr billig, Grösse 44, nur 25 Mark, Wolle mit Baumwolle, und hier ist eine englische Zeitung ... und gibt es nicht jetzt Tennis im Fernsehen?

New words

Learn the **New words** in half the time by using **flash cards**. There are 18 to start you off. Get a friend to make the rest!

gehen *go*
einkaufen *to do the shopping*
müssen / ich muss *must / I must*
heute *today*
Bus *bus*
Zentrum *centre*
Wetter *weather*
Fernsehen *television*
es tut mir Leid *I'm sorry*
zuerst *first*
zu, zum, zur *to, to the*
Geldautomat *cash dispenser*
Post *post office*
Briefmarken *stamps*
Apotheke *chemist's*
Reinigung *dry cleaner's*
Fussball *football*
alle / alles *all*
Kaufhaus *department store*
neu *new*
Koffer *suitcase*
kaufen / gekauft *buy / bought*
Friseur *hairdresser's*
Schuhgeschäft *shoe shop*
Geschäft, Geschäfte *shop, shops*
ach, du meine Güte! *Good grief!*
wann *when*
offen *open*
glauben / ich glaube *believe, think / I believe, I think*
später *later*
zuviel *too much*
Gramm *gram*
Schinken *ham*
Stück *piece*
Käse *cheese*
Kartoffeln *potatoes*
Wiener *Vienna sausages (hot dogs)*
Brot *bread*
Butter *butter*
Ei, Eier *egg, eggs*
Zucker *sugar*
Flasche, Flaschen *bottle, bottles*
Bier *beer*
Wein *wine*
kein Problem *no problem*
gestern *yesterday*
Karstadt a well known chain of department stores
Tüte *bag* (paper or plastic)
mich *me*
sehen / gesehen *see / seen*
genau *exactly*
Grösse *size*
blau *blue*
weiss *white*
Verkäufer *sales assistant*
nett *nice*
so ... wie *as ... as*
wer *who*
dasselbe *the same*
verrückt *crazy*
dies, dieser, diese, dieses *this*
billig *cheap*
Wolle *wool*
Baumwolle *cotton*
Zeitung *newspaper*

TOTAL NEW WORDS: 66
...only 153 words to go!

Good news grammar

1 Remember: *möchten, können, müssen*

When these verbs appear, the other verb goes to the end of the sentence.

Example Wir **müssen** heute viel Bier ... **kaufen.**

2 Good news: shortcut!

Whenever you *would like* or *must* GO somewhere you can drop the word *go*. (But if you do not drop it, that's OK, too.)

Example Wir **müssen** zur Bank. (gehen) Ich **möchte** zu Karstadt. (gehen)

3 Not so bad: the past

Imagine that you are getting married today. You would say: *I do*. If it happened yesterday you would say *I did* or *I have done it.*

When you talk about something that happened before, or in the past in German you use **haben** plus the other verb, slightly changed and often starting with **ge-**.

Example **Wir haben gekauft.** *We bought.*

As in the case of **möchten, können** and **müssen** when you use **haben** the other verb always goes right to the end of the sentence.

Example I *have seen* Tom Cruise. Ich **habe** Tom Cruise ... **gesehen.**
We *bought* a car yesterday. Wir **haben** gestern ein Auto ... **gekauft.**

As you can see: another suspense story! Nobody knows right up to the end *what* we did to the car yesterday... *sold* it? *smashed* it up?

Once you get into the habit of putting the second verb at the end you'll have mastered half of **Instant German** grammar!

On page 70 there's a summary of all **Instant** verbs and verb forms. Whenever you get in a muddle have a quick look there.

4 Some easy extras – *Farben* (colours)

As a reward for the mental acrobatics with verbs here are ten useful words for when you want to change that pink shirt for a green one...

weiss	**schwarz**	**rot**	**blau**	**gelb**	**grün**	**orange**	**rosa**	**grau**	**braun**
white	*black*	*red*	*blue*	*yellow*	*green*	*orange*	*pink*	*grey*	*brown*

Learn by heart

Try to say these eight lines in less than a minute!

Wir müssen heute einkaufen

Wir müssen heute einkaufen – kein Problem!

Aber wo gibt es einen Bus zu den Geschäften?

Ach, du meine Güte! Ich glaube, ich habe nicht genug Geld.

Es tut mir Leid, aber wir müssen zuerst zu einem Geldautomaten.

Wir haben im Supermarkt viel gekauft: Brot, Butter, Schinken und Käse, und zwei Flaschen Wein.

Es war nicht billig: fünfzig Mark, aber der Verkäufer war sehr nett.

The more expression you use when saying it, the easier it will be to remember all the useful bits.

Spot the keys

By now you can say many things in German. But what happens if you ask a question and do not understand the answer – especially if it hits you at the speed of an automatic rifle? The smart way is not to panic, but to listen only for the words you know. Any familiar words which you pick up will provide you with **Key words** – clues to what the other person is saying.

If you have the recording close the book now and listen to the dialogue. Here's an example:

YOU Entschuldigen Sie bitte, wo ist die Post?

ANSWER *Also, dasistganzeinfach. Erstmal* **immer geradeaus bis** *zurnächsten Kreuzung, dabeidem* **grossen roten Haus. Dann links**, *daistein Altersheimundmehrere* **Geschäfte**. *Undgleichdahinter* **rechts** *kommen Siezudem Park* **Platz** *vorder* **Post**.

Although most words run into each other when spoken you should have still managed to pick up:

immer geradeaus – bis – gross – rot – Haus – dann links – Geschäfte – rechts – Platz – Post ... so you should be able to get to the post office!

▶ Let's speak German

Now let's practise again what you have learned. If you have the recording, use it to check your answers. Read the sentences OUT LOUD, one at a time, then translate or answer them OUT LOUD.

1 I am now going to the post office.
2 When are the shops open?
3 I am sorry, but that is too expensive.
4 Where is there a bus to the centre?
5 We ate at Karstadt.
6 Can one buy wine in the supermarket?
7 Shopping without money? No, but with a credit card.
8 I bought everything in the department store.
9 Have you seen the weather on the TV?
10 Good grief, the suitcase is broken!

Answer the following in German using the words in brackets:

11 Haben Sie die Schuhe in Grösse 38? (ja, wir)
12 Haben Sie das Bier im Supermarkt gekauft? (ja, wir)
13 Haben Sie meine Frau gesehen? (nein, wir)
14 Müssen Sie um neun Uhr gehen? (nein, wir)
15 Haben Sie zuviel gegessen? (nein, wir)
16 Was haben Sie gekauft: ein Stück Käse oder Schinken? (Schinken)
17 Wer hat gestern billig gegessen? (ich)
18 Bis wann sind die Geschäfte offen? (acht Uhr)
19 Möchten Sie ein viertel oder ein halbes Kilo Kaffee? (ein halbes)
20 Gibt es einen Bus zum Hotel? (ja)

Answers

1 Ich gehe jetzt zur Post.
2 Wann sind die Geschäfte offen?
3 Es tut mir Leid, aber das ist zu teuer.
4 Wo gibt es einen Bus zum Zentrum?
5 Wir haben bei Karstadt gegessen.
6 Kann man im Supermarkt Wein kaufen?
7 Einkaufen ohne Geld? Nein, aber mit einer Kreditkarte.
8 Ich habe alles im Kaufhaus gekauft.
9 Haben Sie das Wetter im Fernsehen gesehen?
10 Ach, du meine Güte, der Koffer ist kaputt!
11 Ja, wir haben die Schuhe in Grösse 38.
12 Ja, wir haben das Bier im Supermarkt gekauft.
13 Nein, wir haben Ihre Frau nicht gesehen.
14 Nein, wir müssen nicht um neun Uhr gehen.
15 Nein, wir haben nicht zuviel gegessen.
16 Ich habe / Wir haben Schinken gekauft.
17 Ich habe gestern billig gegessen.
18 Die Geschäfte sind bis acht Uhr offen.
19 Ich möchte / Wir möchten ein halbes Kilo Kaffee.
20 Ja, es gibt einen Bus zum Hotel.

Test your progress

Translate these sentences into German, in writing. Before you mark your work check again on the scoring instructions. Enter the result on the Progress chart and be amazed! You are now halfway home, and it will be getting easier all the time!

1. Can you see a sales assistant?
2. Where can we buy something to eat?
3. When must you (go) to the office today? At seven? How terrible!
4. We saw that yesterday on (in the) television.
5. I believe the shops are now open.
6. Is there a department store here or a centre with shops?
7. Excuse me, are you also going to the post office?
8. Where did you buy the English newspaper?
9. Who would like wine, and who would like to drink beer?
10. The weather will be (is) bad tomorrow. That is not nice.
11. That is all? That was cheap.
12. The stamps cost exactly five euros.
13. The cash dispenser is for all credit cards.
14. Are 300 grams (of) cheese too much? No, no problem.
15. There is a new dry cleaner's three minutes from here.
16. Do you have a bag for my shoes, please?
17. I believe I have seen a chemist's here.
18. Good grief, all (the) eggs and three bottles are broken!
19. Can you see that? Is that cotton?
20. Size twelve in England – what is that here?

Check your answers on page 76. And don't forget the Progress chart.

04 week four

Study 35 minutes a day but if you are keen try 40 … 45 …!

Day one

- Read **We are going to eat**.
- Listen to/Read **Wir gehen essen.**
- Read the **New words**. Learn the easy ones.

Day two

- Repeat the dialogue. Learn the harder **New words**.
- Cut out the **Flash words** to help you.

Day three

- Learn all the **New words** until you know them well.
- Read and learn the **Good news grammar**.

Day four

- Cut out and learn the ten **Flash sentences**.
- Listen to/Read **Learn by heart**.

Day five

- Read **Say it simply**.
- Listen to/Read **Let's speak German**.

Day six

- Listen to/Read **Spot the keys**.
- Translate **Test your progress**.

Day seven: Are you keeping your scores above 60%? In that case … Have a good day off!

We are going to eat out

Tom and Kate are still in Stuttgart. Horst Schmidt is inviting them to dinner.

Kate Tom, someone telephoned. He did not say why. The number is on the paper by the telephone book. A Mr Schmidt from Frankfurt.

Tom Oh yes, Horst Schmidt, a good client of the company. I know him well. He is very nice. I have an appointment with him on Thursday. That is an important matter.

Tom (*On the phone*) Hello, good morning, Herr Schmidt. Tom Walker here ... Yes, thank you ... Yes, sure, that is possible ... next week ... of course ... yes, very interesting ... no, we have time ... wonderful ... no, only a few days ... I see ... when? ... at eight o'clock ... at the top by the exit, by the door. Well, until Tuesday, thank you very much, goodbye.

Kate What are we doing on Tuesday?

Tom We are going to eat with Herr Schmidt. In the centre, behind the church. He says the restaurant is new but cosy. Herr Schmidt is in Stuttgart for two days, with Edith and Peter Palmer from our office.

Kate I know Edith Palmer. She is boring and knows everything better. She has a terrible dog. I think I am going to be sick on Tuesday. A heavy cold and pains. The doctor must come...

Tom No, please, that's not on, one cannot do that.

(In the restaurant.)

Waiter The fish is not on the menu, and the dessert today is Apfelstrudel with ice cream or cream.

Horst Mrs Walker, can I help you? Perhaps a soup, and then fish or meat?

Kate I would very much like the steak with salad, please.

Edith I think too much red meat is not good for you, Kate.

Horst Mr Walker, what can we give you? And what would you like to drink? Wine?

Tom I would prefer a beer and then the fried sausage, with potatoes and vegetables, please.

Edith Tom, the vegetables are in cream. I would not like to eat that.

→ Page 46

Wir gehen essen

Tom and Kate are still in Stuttgart. Horst Schmidt is inviting them to dinner.

Kate Tom, jemand hat telefoniert. Er hat nicht gesagt, warum. Die Nummer ist auf dem Papier beim Telefonbuch. Ein Herr Schmidt aus Frankfurt.

Tom Oh, ja, Horst Schmidt, ein guter Kunde von der Firma. Ich kenne ihn gut. Er ist sehr nett. Ich habe Donnerstag einen Termin mit ihm. Das ist eine wichtige Sache.

Tom (*Telefoniert*) Hallo? Guten Morgen, Herr Schmidt. Tom Walker hier ... Ja, danke ... Ja, sicher, das ist möglich ... nächste Woche ... natürlich ... ja, sehr interessant ... nein, wir haben Zeit ... wunderbar ... nein, nur ein paar Tage ... ach so ... wann? ... um acht Uhr ... oben am Ausgang, an der Tür ... Also bis Dienstag, vielen Dank, auf Wiedersehen.

Kate Was machen wir Dienstag?

Tom Wir gehen mit Herrn Schmidt essen. Im Zentrum, hinter der Kirche. Er sagt, das Restaurant ist neu aber gemütlich. Herr Schmidt ist für zwei Tage in Stuttgart, mit Edith und Peter Palmer von unserer Firma.

Kate Ich kenne Edith Palmer. Sie ist langweilig und weiss alles besser. Sie hat einen schrecklichen Hund. Ich glaube, ich bin am Dienstag krank. Eine schwere Erkältung und Schmerzen. Der Arzt muss kommen.

Tom Nein, bitte, das geht nicht, das kann man nicht machen!

(Im Restaurant.)

Kellner Der Fisch ist nicht auf der Speisekarte, und der Nachtisch ist heute Apfelstrudel mit Eis oder Sahne.

Horst Frau Walker, kann ich Ihnen helfen? Vielleicht eine Suppe, und dann Fisch oder Fleisch?

Kate Ich möchte gern das Steak mit Salat, bitte.

Edith Ich glaube, zuviel rotes Fleisch ist nicht gut für Sie, Kate.

Horst Herr Walker, was können wir Ihnen geben? Und was möchten Sie trinken? Wein?

Tom Ich möchte lieber ein Bier und dann die Bratwurst, mit Kartoffeln und Gemüse, bitte.

Edith Tom, das Gemüse ist in Sahne. Ich möchte das nicht essen.

→ Page 47

Horst And you, Mrs Palmer?

Edith A little chicken from the grill, fruit and a glass of water, please.

(Later…)

Horst Are we all ready? It is late. Would anybody like a cup of coffee? Nobody? Good, the bill please.

Edith Oh, Herr Schmidt, can you help me please! How do you say 'doggy bag' in German? I would like a bag for my dog.

Kate But Edith, the dog is in England!

New words

jemand *someone*
er *he*
sagen / gesagt *say / said*
warum *why*
Nummer *number*
auf *on*
Papier *paper*
bei, beim *at, at the*
Buch *book*
Herr *Mr, gentleman*
Kunde *client*
kennen *to know*
ihn, ihm *him*
Donnerstag *Thursday*
Termin *appointment*
wichtig *important*
Sache *matter, thing*
danke *thank you*
sicher *sure, certainly*
möglich *possible*
nächste Woche *next week*
natürlich *of course*
interessant *interesting*
Zeit *time*
wunderbar *wonderful*
ein paar *a few*
ach so *I see*
oben *at the top, upstairs*
an *at*
Ausgang *exit*
Tür *door*
Dienstag *Tuesday*
vielen Dank *thank you very much*
hinter *behind*
Kirche *church*
gemütlich *comfortable, cosy*
unser, unsere *our*
sie weiss / wissen *she knows / know (something)*
Hund *dog*
krank *sick*
schwer *heavy, difficult*
Erkältung *cold*
Schmerzen *pains*
Arzt *doctor*
kommen *come*
das geht nicht *that's not possible, that's not on*
Fisch *fish*
Speisekarte *menu*
Nachtisch *dessert*
Eis *ice cream*
Ihnen *you*
helfen / geholfen *help / helped*
Suppe *soup*
Fleisch *meat*

Horst Und Sie, Frau Palmer?

Edith Ein bisschen Huhn vom Grill, Obst und ein Glas Wasser, bitte.

(Später…)

Horst Sind wir alle fertig? Es ist spät. Möchte jemand eine Tasse Kaffee? Niemand? Gut, die Rechnung, bitte.

Edith Oh, Herr Schmidt, können Sie mir bitte helfen! Wie sagt man auf deutsch 'doggy bag'? Ich möchte eine Tüte für meinen Hund.

Kate Aber Edith, der Hund ist in England!

gern *gladly, very much*
Salat *salad*
geben / gegeben *give/ given*
lieber *rather* (i.e. prefer)
Bratwurst *fried sausage*
Gemüse *vegetables*
Huhn *chicken*
Obst *fruit*
Glas *glass*
Wasser *water*
fertig *ready*
niemand *nobody*
wie sagt man … auf deutsch? *how do you say … in German?*

TOTAL NEW WORDS: 67
…only 86 words to go!

Last easy extras

The days of the week

Montag *Monday*
Dienstag *Tuesday*
Mittwoch *Wednesday*
Donnerstag *Thursday*
Freitag *Friday*
Sonnabend/Samstag *Saturday*
Sonntag *Sunday*

Good news grammar

1 The future: more good news!

In colloquial German there is no difference between: *I am sick* **Ich bin krank** and *I am going to be sick tomorrow* **Ich bin morgen krank.**

So when you are talking about things that are *going to happen*, there's no need to add frills like *shall*, *will*, or *going to*.

2 *Gern* and *lieber*: easy!

If you want to say that you are *enjoying* something, you use **gern:**
Ich helfe Jim gern. Ich spreche gern Deutsch.

If you want to say that you **prefer** doing something you use **lieber:**
Ich helfe lieber Paula. Ich spreche lieber Spanisch.

3 Pronouns: useful

These are the little words which save you repeating the name of the person you are talking about: *Tom said to Kate that **he** was going to meet **her***, as opposed to *Tom said to Kate that Tom was going to meet Kate.*

Here are the personal pronouns you'll learn in **Instant German**:

I	*you*	*he*	*she*	*it*	*we*	*they*	*me*
ich	**Sie/Ihnen**	**er**	**sie**	**es**	**wir**	**sie**	**mich/mir**

him	*her*	*us*	*them*
ihn/ihm	**sie/ihr**	**uns**	**sie/Ihnen**

This may look like a bit of a minefield, especially when there are two choices for the same word. But amazingly, you will learn to pick the right one most of the time.

4 The third person (just like in English)

When you are talking about another person or about something, you often have to change the verb, just like you do in English.

Example I *eat* – Tom *eats*. Ich **esse** – Tom **isst.**
I *have* – it *has*. Ich **habe** – es **hat.**

In Week 2, you learned about dropping the **n** when saying **ich,** so this is just another small step.

When in doubt, remember you'll find all **Instant** verbs on page 70.

Learn by heart

Pretend this is a one-sided telephone call by a rather opinionated person. When you know it act it out in less than 50 seconds.

Möchten Sie mit mir essen gehen?

Möchten Sie Freitag abend mit mir essen gehen?
Ich kenne ein sehr gemütliches Restaurant.
Man kann da viele gute Sachen essen, und der Wein ist wunderbar.
Nein, Sie möchten nicht? Warum nicht? Ich bin sehr interessant!
Sie kennen mich nicht?
Aber sicher, Sie sehen mich immer im Fernsehen: Ich mache das Wetter.
Sie können nicht? Warum nicht?
Sie haben einen wichtigen Termin?
Das ist nicht möglich!

Say it simply

When people want to speak German but don't dare it's usually because they are trying to *translate* what they want to say from English into German. But because they don't know some of the words they give up!

With **Instant German** you work around the words you don't know with the words you know. And 350 words is enough to say anything!

It may not be very elegant – but who cares? You are *communicating*!

Here are two examples showing you how to say things simply.

1 You need to change your flight from Tuesday to Friday.
Say it simply: Wir können nicht Dienstag fliegen, wir möchten Freitag fliegen. *or*: **Dienstag ist nicht gut für uns. Wir möchten den Flug am Freitag.**

2 This time your friend has just broken the heel of her only pair of shoes. You have to catch a train and need some help now.
Say it simply: Entschuldigen Sie, der Schuh hier ist kaputt. Gibt es hier ein Geschäft, wo man das sehr schnell repariert?

Let's speak German

Here are ten sentences as a warm-up, and then on to greater things!

1 Who has said that?
2 I don't know why.
3 Can I help you?
4 I believe we have time later.
5 I enjoy driving to Hamburg.
6 He would like to know that.
7 Work on Sunday? That's not on!
8 Can I give you my number?
9 I prefer to eat chicken.
10 Yes, sure, I have an appointment for you.

Now pretend you are in Germany with friends who do not speak German. They will want you to ask people things in German. They will say: *Please ask him…*

11 if he knows Edith Palmer.
12 if he is going to eat with us on Tuesday.
13 if she would like meat or fish and potatoes.
14 if they have an appointment today.
15 if they know where the restaurant is.

Now they ask you to tell people things. This time they use some words you don't know, so you have to use your **Instant** words. They say: *Please tell her…*

16 that the soup is stone cold.
17 that we are unfortunately in a rush now.
18 that we would like to have a meal with them.
19 that I am a vegetarian.
20 that next week will suit us.

Answers

1 Wer hat das gesagt?
2 Ich weiss nicht warum.
3 Kann ich Ihnen helfen?
4 Ich glaube, wir haben später Zeit.
5 Ich fahre gern nach Hamburg.
6 Er möchte das gern wissen.
7 Sonntag arbeiten? Das geht nicht!
8 Kann ich Ihnen meine Nummer geben?
9 Ich esse lieber Huhn.
10 Ja sicher, ich habe einen Termin für Sie.
11 Kennen Sie Edith Palmer?
12 Essen Sie Dienstag mit uns?
13 Möchten Sie Fleisch oder Fisch und Kartoffeln?
14 Haben Sie heute einen Termin?
15 Wissen Sie, wo das Restaurant ist?
16 Die Suppe ist leider kalt.
17 Wir haben jetzt leider keine Zeit.
18 Wir möchten (gern) mit Ihnen essen.
19 Er / sie isst kein Fleisch.
20 Nächste Woche ist gut für uns.

Spot the keys

Now you are in a department store and ask the sales assistant if the black shoes you fancy were also available in size 39:

YOU Entschuldigen Sie, haben Sie diese Schuhe auch in Grösse 39?

She said **nein** then **einen Moment bitte** and went into the stockroom. When she came back this is what she said:

ANSWER *Alsoichhabeebennoch inunserem Lager angerufendass-dienochmalnachkucken aberdiehabendie* **Schuhe** *nur nochin* **braun**. *Aberichweissaus Erfahrungdassdiese Markeoft* **sehr gross** *ausfälltundichmeine* **Grösse achtunddreissig** *wäreeventuell* **gross genug**.

Size 39 was only available in brown but size 38 should be big enough.

Test your progress

1 I am sure our appointment was (on) Tuesday.
2 Today? No, that is not possible. Unfortunately we do not have time.
3 I must buy a few things for my friends.
4 Can you help me please? I would like the number of the doctor.
5 Do you know where there is a good restaurant?
6 I believe the church is very interesting, but nobody would like to see it.
7 We would like to fly next Monday evening.
8 Can you give me the menu please?
9 Have you given him your papers?
10 Can one buy fruit and vegetables here?
11 Do you know his new book?
12 It was wonderful, thank you very much for the nice evening!
13 Why must you see my credit card?
14 The two weeks on the QE II were a little boring.
15 You see the cash dispenser upstairs at the exit, by the door.
16 We eat chicken or fried sausage – the fish is too expensive.
17 How does one say in German…?
18 Do you know where there is a bus here?
19 My husband likes going to Texas, but I prefer going to Arizona.
20 They did not say where this cosy restaurant was.

There were eight split verbs in this test. Did you spot them? Check your answers on page 76. Another brilliant score on the chart.

Well on the way

After four weeks you are well on the way, and as a reward for all your hard work here's a bit of light relief – a multiple choice quiz. Some of the answers are in German so you have to be smart. But you only need to score five out of ten for a gold star!

1 What would you expect to be offered in Germany for breakfast?
a Salami **b** Schinken **c** Käse **d** Orangenmarmelade

2 How do you say 'half past twelve' in German?
a halb zwölf **b** halb eins **c** halb elf **d** halb nach zwölf

3 How would Herr Schmidt and Frau Schulze address each other after having been good neighbours for ten years?
a Helmut and Karin **b** Liebling **c** Herr Schmidt and Frau Schulze

4 How do you say and spell 'sales assistant' in German?
a verkaufer **b** Verkeufer **c** Verkäufer **d** Kellner

5 When do you exchange Christmas presents in Germany?
a Heiligabend (24th) **b** am ersten Weihnachtstag (25th), morgens **c** am ersten Weihnachtstag, abends

6 What's wrong? Ich habe gekauft den Wein am Sonntag bei Karstadt.
a gekauft muss ans Ende **b** nichts **c** alles

7 What does 'es gibt' mean?
a It gives **b** does he give? **c** there is, there are

8 What is 'New Year's Eve' in German, and what happens at midnight?
a Ostern/nichts **b** Sylvester/grosses Feuerwerk
c Pfingsten/arbeiten

9 How do you say in German 'I am sorry'?
a Es tut mir Leid **b** ach du meine Güte **c** kein Problem

10 What do Germans do when they meet?
a lachen **b** küssen **c** geben sich die Hand **d** nichts

Answers:

1 a, b, c **2** b **3** c **4** c **5** a **6** a, c Stores are not open on Sunday. **7** a, c **8** b **9** a **10** c

05 week five

How about 15 minutes on the train / tube / bus, 10 minutes on the way home and 20 minutes before switching on the television ...?

Day one

- Read **On the move**.
- Listen to/Read **Unterwegs**.
- Read the **New words**. Learn 15+.

Day two

- Repeat **Unterwegs** and **New words**.
- Cut out the **Flash words** and get stuck in.

Day three

- Test yourself to perfection on all the **New words**.
- Read and learn **Good news grammar**.

Day four

- Cut out and learn the ten **Flash sentences**.
- Listen to/Read **Learn by heart**.

Day five

- Listen to/Read **Let's speak German**.
- Listen to/Read **Spot the keys**.

Day six

- Translate **Test your progress**.

Day seven: I bet you don't want a day off ... but I insist!

On the move

Tom and Kate are now travelling through Bavaria by train, bus and hire car. They talk to Helga, the ticket clerk at the station, to Jim in the train and later to Heino, the bus driver.

(At the station.)

Tom Two tickets please to Lake Starnberg.

Helga Thereandback?

Tom There and what? Can you speak slowly, please?

Helga There – and – back?

Tom Only there, please. When does the train go, and where (from)?

Helga Nine forty-five, platform eight.

Kate Quick, Tom, here are two seats in the non-smoking. Oh, someone is smoking there. Excuse me, you cannot smoke here, because this is 'non smoking'. Smoking is forbidden here.

Jim Sorry, I don't understand. I only speak English.

(At the bus stop.)

Kate On a Sunday the bus does not come often. We have to wait for 20 minutes. Tom, here are my postcards and a letter. There is a letterbox down there. I am taking a few photos. The lake is so beautiful in the sun.

Tom Kate, quickly, two buses are coming. Both are blue. This one is full. We take the other one. *(In the bus.)* Two to Munich please.

Heino This bus goes to Lake Starnberg only.

Tom But we are at Lake Starnberg.

Heino Yes, yes, but this is the bus for the Starnberg hospital.

(In the car.)

Tom Here comes our car. Only 100 Deutschmarks for three days. I am very pleased.

Kate I do not like the car. I think it was so cheap because it is very old. I hope that we are not going to have problems.

Tom The first car was too expensive, the second one too big. This was the last. *(Later.)* Where are we? The map has gone. On the left is a petrol station and a stop for the underground and on the right is a school. Quickly!

→ Page 58

Unterwegs

Tom and Kate are now travelling through Bavaria by train, bus and hire car. They talk to Helga, the ticket clerk at the station, to Jim in the train and later to Heino, the bus driver.

(Am Bahnhof.)

Tom Zwei Fahrkarten bitte zum Starnberger See.

Helga Hinundzurück?

Tom Hin und was? Können Sie bitte langsam sprechen?

Helga Hin – und – zurück?

Tom Nur hin, bitte. Wann fährt der Zug und wo?

Helga Neun Uhr fünfundvierzig, Gleis acht.

Kate Schnell, Tom, hier sind zwei Plätze im Nichtraucher. Oh, da raucht jemand. Entschuldigen Sie, Sie können hier nicht rauchen, denn dies ist kein Raucher. Rauchen ist hier verboten.

Jim Sorry, I don't understand. Ich spreche only English.

(An der Bushaltestelle.)

Kate Am Sonntag kommt der Bus nicht oft. Wir müssen zwanzig Minuten warten. Tom, hier sind meine Karten und ein Brief. Da unten ist ein Briefkasten. Ich mache ein paar Fotos. Der See ist so schön in der Sonne.

Tom Kate, schnell, zwei Busse kommen. Beide sind blau. Dieser ist voll. Wir nehmen den anderen. *(Im Bus.)* Zweimal nach München bitte.

Heino Dieser Bus fährt nur zum Starnberger See.

Tom Aber wir sind am Starnberger See.

Heino Ja, ja, aber dies ist der Bus zum Starnberger Krankenhaus.

(Im Auto.)

Tom Hier kommt unser Auto. Nur hundert Mark für drei Tage. Ich bin sehr zufrieden.

Kate Das Auto gefällt mir nicht. Ich glaube es war so billig, weil es sehr alt ist. Ich hoffe, dass wir keine Probleme haben...

Tom Das erste Auto war zu teuer und das zweite zu gross. Dies war das letzte. *(Später.)* Wo sind wir? Die Karte ist weg. Links sind eine Tankstelle und eine U-Bahn Haltestelle, und rechts ist eine Schule. Schnell!

→ Page 59

Kate The main road is at the traffic light. If we go to the end we'll come to the motorway. Perhaps three kilometres. *(On the motorway.)* Why does the car go so slowly? Do we have enough petrol? How many litres? Do we have oil? Is the engine hot? I think the car 'has had it'. Where is the mobile phone? Where is the number of the workshop? Where is my bag?

Tom Kate, these questions are making me mad. And here comes the rain! And why are the police behind us?

New words

unterwegs *on the move*
Bahnhof *(railway) station*
Fahrkarte *ticket*
hin und zurück *there and back, return (ticket)*
langsam *slow, slowly*
sprechen / gesprochen *speak / spoken*
Zug *train*
Gleis *track, platform*
schnell *quick, quickly*
Nichtraucher *non-smoker, non-smoking (compartment)*
rauchen *smoke*
denn *because*
Raucher *smoker, smoking (compartment)*
verboten *forbidden*
Haltestelle *stop*
oft *often*
warten / gewartet *wait / waited*
Karte *card, postcard, map*
Brief *letter*
(da) unten *down (there), at the bottom*
Kasten *box*
Foto *photo*
See *lake, sea*
Sonne *sun*
beide *both*
voll *full*
nehmen / genommen *take / taken*
anderer, andere *other, other one*
zweimal *twice*
Krankenhaus *hospital*
Auto *car*
Tag, Tage *day, days*
zufrieden *content, happy*
es gefällt mir nicht *I don't like it (it pleases me not)*
weil *because*
alt *old*
hoffen *hope*
dass *that*
erste *first*
zweite *second*
letzte *last*
weg *gone*
Tankstelle *petrol station*
U-Bahn *underground*
Schule *school*
Hauptstrasse *main road*
Ampel *traffic light*
wenn *if, when*
Ende *end*
Autobahn *motorway*
Kilometer *kilometre*

Kate Die Hauptstrasse ist bei der Ampel. Wenn wir bis zum Ende fahren, kommen wir zur Autobahn. Vielleicht drei Kilometer. *(Auf der Autobahn.)* Warum fährt das Auto so langsam? Haben wir genug Benzin? Wieviel Liter? Haben wir Öl? Ist der Motor heiss? Ich glaube das Auto ist kaputt. Wo ist das Handy? Wo ist die Nummer von der Werkstatt? Wo ist meine Tasche?

Tom Kate, diese Fragen machen mich verrückt. Und hier kommt der Regen. Und warum ist die Polizei hinter uns?

Benzin *petrol*
Liter *litre*
Öl *oil*
Motor *engine*
heiss *hot*
Handy *mobile phone*
Werkstatt *workshop, garage*
Tasche *bag*
Regen *rain*
Polizei *police, police station*
uns *us*

TOTAL NEW WORDS: 62
...only 24 words to go!

Es gefällt mir 'I like it' means literally: *it pleases me*
Es gefällt mir nicht 'I do not like it' *it pleases me not*

Das Auto gefällt mir. *I like the car. (The car pleases me.)*
Das Auto gefällt uns nicht. *We do not like the car. (The car does not please us.)*

Good news grammar!

1 *Dass* (that), *weil* (because), *wenn* (if, when)

- Ich hoffe, **dass** wir keine Probleme **haben.**
- Das Auto ist so billig, **weil** es so alt **ist.**
- Wir haben kein Geld mehr, **wenn** wir das Haus **gekauft haben.**

Can you see that after **dass, weil** or **wenn** the verb goes to the end? And **haben gekauft** does an extra twist, becoming **gekauft haben**! Don't kill the messenger!

If you get it wrong – it's not a problem.

Good news: another word for *because* is **denn.** No change after **denn:** Das Auto ist billig, **denn es ist alt.** Good old **denn**! Use it!

2 Another twist

Here's a harmless-looking sentence: *First we eat fish*. This should be: Zuerst **wir essen** Fisch. But instead it is: Zuerst **essen wir** Fisch.

This sentence doesn't start with the subject (*we*), so the verb (**essen**) has rushed into second place. *First eat we fish*. Remember: ... **da raucht** jemand. **Am Sonntag kommt** der Bus? But if you say **Am Sonntag der Bus kommt** it's near enough!

Learn by heart

Here's a dialogue between someone who pranged the car and someone else who is getting suspicious! Try to say the ten lines like a prize-winning one-act play. I challenge you to 45 seconds.

Das Auto ist nur ein bisschen kaputt!

Können wir morgen zum Tennis gehen?
Jemand hat mir Karten gegeben.
Ich möchte die zwei neuen Amerikaner sehen.
Und können wir die U-Bahn nehmen?
Oder besser den Bus, weil er genau zum Tennisplatz fährt.

Bus? U-Bahn? Warum? Die Sache gefällt mir nicht.
Wir haben unten ein schönes Auto.

Ja, also ... ich habe nicht gesehen, dass die Ampel rot war...
Aber das Auto ist nur ein bisschen kaputt!

Let's speak German

Here's your ten-point warm up: I give you an answer and you ask me a question, as if you did not hear the words in **bold** very well.

Example Steffie ist **hier**. *Question* **Wo** ist Steffie?

1 Das Handy ist **in meiner Tasche**.
2 Die **Autobahn** ist da unten.
3 Der Bus kommt **in zwanzig Minuten**.
4 **Tom** möchte mit Herrn Schmidt sprechen.
5 Hin und zurück nach Köln kostet **30 Mark**.
6 Das Haus gefällt mir nicht, **weil** es sehr alt ist.
7 Sie kommen **mit dem Auto** nach England.
8 Ich habe **die Ampel** nicht gesehen.
9 **Ja**, das Hotel gefällt mir.
10 **Nein**, ich bin mit der Schule nicht zufrieden.

Now answer, starting with **ja** and **ich**:

11 Kennen Sie die neue Autobahn?
12 Nehmen Sie diesen Bus?
13 Gehen Sie jetzt zum Bahnhof?
14 Gefällt Ihnen der See?
15 Können Sie die Haltestelle sehen?

Here are five things you want to refer to but you don't know what they are called in German. Explain them using the words you know.

16 your parents-in-law
17 central heating
18 a headache
19 a teacher
20 a kennel

Answers

1 Wo ist das Handy?
2 Was ist da unten?
3 Wann kommt der Bus?
4 Wer möchte mit Herrn Schmidt sprechen?
5 Wieviel kostet es nach Köln?
6 Warum gefällt Ihnen das Haus nicht?
7 Wie kommen sie nach England?
8 Was haben Sie nicht gesehen?
9 Gefällt Ihnen das Hotel?
10 Sind Sie mit der Schule zufrieden?
11 Ja, ich kenne die neue Autobahn.
12 Ja, ich nehme diesen Bus.
13 Ja, ich gehe jetzt zum Bahnhof.
14 Ja, der See gefällt mir.
15 Ja, ich kann die Haltestelle sehen.
16 Die Eltern von meinem Mann.
17 Es macht alle Zimmer im Haus warm.
18 Schmerzen hier oben.
19 Der Mann oder die Frau in der Schule. Sie arbeiten mit den Kindern.
20 Ein Haus für Hunde, wenn wir Urlaub haben.

Spot the keys

This time you are planning a trip in the country and want to have some idea what the weather will be like. This is what you would ask:

YOU Entschuldigen Sie, können Sie mir bitte sagen, was für Wetter wir morgen haben?

ANSWER *Ja,* **ich weiss nicht**, *ob die letzte* **Wetter** *vorhersage im* **Fernsehen** *stimmt,* **aber** *danachsolldas Tiefdruckgebiet* **langsam** *abziehen, undessoll* **morgen warm** *werden, alsoüber* **fünfundzwanzig** *Grad* **aber** *eventuellkriegenwirdoch wieder* **Regen am Abend**.

He isn't sure but according to the TV something slow is happening(?) and it will be warm tomorrow – 25°C – but with rain again in the evening.

Test your progress

Translate into German.

1 I don't like this bag, the other bag was better.
2 How much does the ticket cost – return?
3 What did you say? Can you speak slowly, please?
4 I know that petrol is cheaper in America.
5 It is forbidden to smoke in the underground.
6 I cannot wait, I have a second appointment at eleven o'clock.
7 Is this box for letters? A yellow letterbox?
8 Hello, we are 30 km from Hanover, is that the garage?
9 Which is faster: the train, or the car on the motorway?
10 It is very hot this week. I would rather (have) a little rain.
11 He did not see the traffic light, and now they are both in hospital.
12 I saw her twice at the petrol station today. Her car drinks petrol!
13 Where is there a dry cleaner's? I have oil on my Armani T-shirt.
14 We live behind the main road, exactly at the bus stop.
15 We are at the police station because our mobile phone has gone.
16 The tickets are cheaper if you buy them now.
17 I like your car. Was it very expensive?
18 Can you help us please? Where can one eat here by the lake?

If you know all your words you should score over 90%!

06 week six

This is your last week! Need I say more?

Day one

- Read **In the airport.**
- Listen to/Read **Im Flughafen.**
- Read the **New words** (only 24!).

Day two

- Repeat **Im Flughafen** and learn all the **New words.**
- Start working with the **Flash sentences.**

Day three

- Test yourself on the **Flash sentences.**
- Listen to/Read **Learn by heart.**

Day four

- No more **Grammar!** Have a look at the summary.
- Read **Say it simply.**

Day five

- Listen to/Read **Spot the keys.**
- Listen to/Read **Let's speak German.**

Day six

- Your last **Test your progress!** Go for it!

Day seven

Congratulations!

You have successfully completed the course and can now speak

Instant German!

In the airport

Tom and Kate are on their way back to Birmingham. They are in the departure lounge at Frankfurt airport.

Tom On Monday we have to work. Terrible! I would like to go to Italy now or fly from here to Hawaii. My company can wait, and nobody knows where I am.

Kate And what are the people in **my** office going to say? They wait for two days and then they'll phone and speak to my mother. I am sure she'll give them the number of our mobile phone. And then?

Tom Yes, yes, I know. Well, perhaps at Christmas, a week in the snow or on a boat to Madeira. I'll go and buy a newspaper downstairs ... Kate! Here is Klaus Becker!

Klaus Hello! How are you? What are you doing here? This is my wife Nancy. Are your holidays finished? How was it?

Kate Germany was wonderful. We have seen a lot and eaten too much! We now know Bavaria and the Black Forest well.

Klaus Next year you must go to the Rhine. Mrs Walker, my wife would like to buy a book for our computer. Could you perhaps go with her and help her? And Mr Walker, you have a newspaper. Could you give me the *Sport* please? And then would you like to have a Schnaps?

(At the airport kiosk.)

Kate I see nothing here. What I see is not right. Are you also flying to England?

Nancy No, we are flying to Hamburg. Klaus's mother lives there. She had our children for two weeks. A boy and three girls. We are coming back by train tomorrow. That is cheaper.

Kate Your husband works at the Deutsche Bank?

Nancy Yes, his job is interesting but the money is not good. Our VW is nine years old and we have a small old flat. We had a lot to repair this year. My parents and my girlfriend are in the USA and we write a lot of letters. I would very much like to fly to America but that costs too much money.

→ Page 68

▶ Im Flughafen

Tom and Kate are on their way home to Birmingham. They are in the departure lounge at Frankfurt airport.

Tom Montag müssen wir arbeiten. Schrecklich! Ich möchte jetzt nach Italien fahren oder von hier nach Hawaii fliegen. Meine Firma kann warten, und niemand weiss, wo ich bin.

Kate Und was sagen die Leute in **meiner** Firma? Sie warten zwei Tage und dann telefonieren sie und sprechen mit meiner Mutter. Sie gibt ihnen sicher die Nummer von unserem Handy. Und dann?

Tom Ja, ja, ich weiss. Also vielleicht Weihnachten eine Woche im Schnee oder mit einem Schiff nach Madeira... Ich gehe unten eine Zeitung kaufen ... Kate! Hier ist Klaus Becker!

Klaus Hallo! Wie geht's? Was machen Sie hier? Dies ist meine Frau, Nancy. Ist Ihr Urlaub zuende? Wie war es?

Kate Deutschland war wunderbar. Wir haben viel gesehen und zuviel gegessen. Wir kennen Bayern und den Schwarzwald jetzt gut.

Klaus Nächstes Jahr müssen Sie an den Rhein fahren. Frau Walker, meine Frau möchte ein Buch für unseren Computer kaufen. Können Sie vielleicht mit ihr gehen und ihr helfen? Und Herr Walker, Sie haben eine Zeitung. Können Sie mir bitte den *Sport* geben? Und möchten Sie dann einen Schnaps trinken?

(Am Kiosk vom Flughafen.)

Kate Ich sehe hier nichts. Was ich sehe, ist nicht richtig.

Fliegen Sie auch nach England?

Nancy Nein, wir fliegen nach Hamburg. Die Mutter von Klaus wohnt da. Sie hatte unsere Kinder für zwei Wochen. Ein Junge und drei Mädchen. Wir kommen morgen mit dem Zug zurück. Das ist billiger.

Kate Ihr Mann arbeitet bei der Deutschen Bank?

Nancy Ja, sein Job ist interessant, aber das Geld ist nicht gut. Unser VW ist neun Jahre alt, und wir haben eine kleine alte Wohnung. Wir hatten dieses Jahr viel zu reparieren. Meine Eltern und meine Freundin sind in den USA, und wir schreiben viele Briefe. Ich möchte gern nach Amerika fliegen, aber das kostet zu viel Geld.

→ Page 69

Kate	But you have a beautiful house in Mallorca.
Nancy	A house in Mallorca? I have never been to Mallorca. When we have a holiday, we go to the Ruhrgebiet to a friend.
Tom	Kate, come, we must (go) to our flight. Goodbye! ... What is the matter, Kate? What did Mrs Becker say?
Kate	Wait, Tom, wait!

New words

Flughafen *airport*
Leute *people*
Mutter *mother*
ihnen *them*
Weihnachten *Christmas*
Schnee *snow*
Schiff *ship*
wie geht's? *how are you?*
zuende *finished, over*
Deutschland *Germany*
ihr *her*
nichts *nothing*
richtig *right*
wohnen *live*
sie hatte / hatten *she had / they had*
Junge *boy*
Mädchen *girl*
sein *his*
Wohnung *apartment, flat*
schreiben *write*
nie *never*
Ruhrgebiet *industrial area of Germany*
Flug *flight*
was ist los? *what is the matter?*

TOTAL NEW WORDS: 24
TOTAL GERMAN WORDS LEARNED: 358
EXTRA WORDS: 65

GRAND TOTAL: 423

Kate	Aber Sie haben ein schönes Haus auf Mallorca.
Nancy	Ein Haus auf Mallorca? Ich war nie auf Mallorca. Wenn wir Urlaub haben, fahren wir ins Ruhrgebiet zu einem Freund.
Tom	Kate, komm, wir müssen zu unserem Flug. Auf Wiedersehen! Was ist los, Kate? Was hat Frau Becker gesagt?
Kate	Warte, Tom, warte…!

Learn by heart

This is your last dialogue to learn by heart. Give it your best!

You now have six prize-winning party pieces, and a large store of everyday sayings which will be very useful.

Auf Wiedersehen

Kate Herr Schmidt, Kate Walker hier, vom Flughafen Frankfurt.
Ja, unser Urlaub ist leider zuende und unser Geld auch.
Vielen Dank für den schönen Abend!
Tom möchte mit Ihnen sprechen, auf Wiedersehen!

Tom Hallo Horst!... Was? Sie kaufen beide? Meine Firma hat Ihr E-mail? Das ist wunderbar. Vielen Dank!
Nächstes Jahr?... Kate möchte nach Italien, aber ich komme lieber nach Deutschland.
Mit Edith Palmer? Ach du meine Güte, nein, nein!
Unser Flugzeug wartet. Also ... auf Wiedersehen!

Good news grammar

Here is a summary of all 32 **Instant** verbs and verb forms.

If you are brave why not test yourself? Cover up the three columns on the right and see how many you can remember. Do you know the meaning of the word and how to say **ich…**, **er…** or the past?

Basic form			Past
Sie / wir / sie (they)	ich	er / sie (she) / es	
arbeiten	arbeite	arbeitet	gearbeitet
einkaufen	kaufe ein	kauft ein	eingekauft
essen	esse	isst	gegessen
fahren	fahre	fährt	
fliegen	fliege	fliegt	
geben	gebe	gibt	gegeben
gehen	gehe	geht	
glauben	glaube	glaubt	geglaubt
haben	habe	hat	gehabt, *or* hatten, hatte
helfen	helfe	hilft	geholfen
hoffen	hoffe	hofft	gehofft
kaufen	kaufe	kauft	gekauft
kennen	kenne	kennt	gekannt
können	kann	kann	gekonnt
kommen	komme	kommt	
kosten	koste	kostet	gekostet
machen	mache	macht	gemacht
möchten	möchte	möchte	gemocht
müssen	muss	muss	gemusst
nehmen	nehme	nimmt	genommen
rauchen	rauche	raucht	geraucht
reparieren	repariere	repariert	repariert
sagen	sage	sagt	gesagt
schreiben	schreibe	schreibt	geschrieben
sehen	sehe	sieht	gesehen
sein / sind	bin	ist	*use:* war, waren
sprechen	spreche	spricht	gesprochen
telefonieren	telefoniere	telefoniert	telefoniert
trinken	trinke	trinkt	getrunken
warten	warte	wartet	gewartet
wissen	weiss	weiss	gewusst
wohnen	wohne	wohnt	gewohnt

Where you see a gap the verb is rather irregular. So work around it or use **war** or **waren** which are good stand-bys.

Say it simply

Here are two more exercises to practise using plain language:

1 You have just hired a car and notice a scratch on the left, behind the door. You want to report it so as not to get the bill for it later.

2 You are at the airport, about to catch your flight home when you realize that you have left some clothes behind in the room of your hotel. You phone the hotel's housekeeper to ask her to send the things on to you.

What would you say? Say it then write it down. Then see page 79.

Spot the keys

Here are two final practice rounds. If you have the recording close the book now. Find the **Key words** and try to get the gist of it. Then check on page 79.

1 This is what you might ask a taxi driver:

YOU Wieviel Minuten ist es zum Flughafen und wieviel kostet es?

ANSWER *Es kommt darauf an, wann Sie fahren. Normalerweise dauert es zwanzig Minuten, aber wenn wir in den Verkehr kommen und die Bleichenbrücke ist dann völl verstopft, müssen Sie mit einer dreiviertel Stunde rechnen. Den Preis können Sie am Meter ablesen. Normalerweise liegt er so zwischen dreissig und fünfunddreissig Mark.*

2 While in the departure lounge of the airport you hear someone raving about something. Identify **Key words** and guess where they have been. The answer is on page 79.

... und mein Mann hat auch gleich gesagt, es gefällt ihm weit aus besser hier. Und die Leute waren gar nicht so reserviert, wie man immer sagt, sondern sehr nett und weitaus höflicher als bei uns. Das Hotel lag direkt am See, und bei dem wunderbaren Wetter sind wir viel gewandert oder mit dem Auto durch die schöne Landschaft gefahren. Es gab da so viel interessantes zu sehen. Auch das Essen, wirklich gut. Also nächstes Jahr gehen wir garantiert zurück nach...

Let's speak German

Here's a five-point warm up. Answer these questions using the words in brackets.

1 Hat er die Wohnung in Marbella gekauft? (Ja, Montag)
2 Wieviel Jahre haben Sie bei BMW gearbeitet? (drei)
3 Wann haben Sie mit Ihrer Firma gesprochen? (gestern)
4 Warum müssen Sie Ihr Auto immer reparieren? (weil, alt)
5 Hat er zuerst bei seiner Mutter gewohnt? (nein, bei seiner Freundin)

In your last exercise you are going to interpret again, this time telling your German friend what others have said in English.

Each time say the whole sentence OUT LOUD, translating the English words in brackets. Remember: after **wenn, dass** and **weil** all verbs go to the end of the sentence!

6 Jemand sagt, Sie sind verrückt,... (if you buy this old flat)
7 Jemand sagt, es gefällt ihm nicht,... (if you come too late)
8 Jemand sagt, es ist kaputt,... (if you have no hot water)
9 Meine Freundin hat gesagt,... (that our holiday is over)
10 Sie hat auch gesagt,... (that we come back next year)
11 Meine Frau möchte sagen,... (that she has a cold)
12 Mein Mann sagt, er kann nicht kommen,... (because he works on a ship)
13 Er kann auch nicht kommen,... (because he is often sick)
14 Mein Freund sagt,... (that you are very beautiful)
15 Er sagt auch,... (that he would like your telephone number)

Answers

1 Ja, er hat Montag die Wohnung in Marbella gekauft.
2 Ich habe drei Jahre bei BMW gearbeitet.
3 Ich habe gestern mit meiner Firma gesprochen.
4 Ich muss mein Auto immer reparieren, weil es sehr alt ist.
5 Nein, er hat zuerst bei seiner Freundin gewohnt.
6 wenn Sie diese alte Wohnung kaufen.
7 wenn Sie zu spät kommen.
8 wenn sie kein heisses Wasser haben.
9 dass unser Urlaub zuende ist.
10 dass wir nächstes Jahr zurück kommen.
11 dass sie eine Erkältung hat.
12 weil er auf einem Schiff arbeitet.
13 weil er oft krank ist.
14 dass Sie sehr schön sind.
15 dass er Ihre Telefonnummer möchte.

Now do it once more – as quickly as you can.

Test your progress

I have put a lot into this last test – all 32 **Instant** verbs! But don't panic – it looks worse than it is. Go for it – you'll do brilliantly!

Translate into German:

1 I enjoy writing letters because I have a new computer.
2 How are you? What is the matter? Can I help you?
3 How many boring people from the office are coming?
4 I do not have the number of her mobile, I am sorry.
5 I like the Black Forest. We had a lot of snow there last year.
6 The second case is in the bus. Can you take the brown bag?
7 How many cards did you write (at) Christmas?
8 That's crazy: I believe somebody has eaten my steak!
9 Why did you not telephone? We waited until yesterday.
10 Quickly! Have you seen a taxi? My plane is waiting.
11 Don't you know that? The airport is always open – day and night.
12 It is important that you are happy with your holiday.
13 I worked on a boat and was never seasick.
14 Did you see me in the newspaper? ... without shoes?
15 Your mother is very nice and makes wonderful applecake.
16 Do you live in a house or a flat in Germany?
17 We must both work. Three boys and two girls cost a lot of money.
18 We hope the garage can repair that.
19 I know him. He always goes shopping with his dog.
20 Who said one cannot smoke here?
21 We fly to Dallas. Then we take a car and drive to Las Vegas.
22 I would like to speak with the sales assistant. He did not give me a receipt.
23 We drank your wine but we have bought two new bottles.
24 I am sorry, but **Instant German** is now finished.

Check your answers on page 78. Then enter a final excellent score on the Progress chart and write out your **Certificate**.

How to score

From a total of 100%

- Subtract 1% for each wrong or missing word.
- Subtract 1% for wrong form of verb. E.g. **Ich gehen; wir hat gekauft.**
- Subtract 1% if you forgot to split the two verbs in a sentence.
  E.g. **Ich möchte kaufen einen Hund. Ich habe gesehen ein Taxi.**

There are no penalties for:

- wrong use of: **der, die, das, dem, den, ein, eine, einem, einen, diesem,** etc.
- wrong ending of word, example: **mit Herr Schmidt; in der gross Tüte.**
- wrong choice of very similar words such as **zu / nach** or **an / bei.**
- wrong word order, example: **Morgen wir kommen zurück mit dem Zug** (should be **Wir kommen morgen mit dem Zug zurück**).
- wrong spelling, as long as you can say the word!

100% LESS YOUR PENALTIES WILL GIVE YOU YOUR WEEKLY SCORE

Week 1

Test your progress

1 Mein Name ist Peter Smith.
2 Guten Tag, wir sind Helen und Elke.
3 Ich bin auch aus Hamburg.
4 Ich war im Oktober in Frankfurt.

5 Meine Frau und ich waren drei Jahre in Amerika.
6 Wir fliegen immer im Juni nach Berlin.
7 Wie war Ihr Urlaub in England?
8 Entschuldigen Sie bitte, was machen Sie jetzt in London?
9 Sind Sie Frau Becker aus Bonn?
10 Das Haus in Hannover ist für meine Kinder.
11 Einen Moment bitte, ich habe das Geld.
12 Gibt es hier ein Telefon? Nein, leider nicht.
13 Ich bin ohne meine Frau in England.
14 Wie gross ist Ihre Firma?
15 Kostet ein Mercedes viel Geld?
16 England ist leider nicht schön im Februar.
17 Udo hat eine Freundin im Reisebüro.
18 Der Tag in Holland war langweilig.
19 Mein Job ist sehr gut, aber Urlaub ist besser.
20 Meine zwei Kinder haben viel Geld.

YOUR SCORE: ___ %

Correct those answers which differ from ours. Then read them out loud twice.

Week 2

Test your progress

1 Ich trinke viel Bier.
2 Wieviel kostet das Frühstück, bitte?
3 Gibt es ein Reisebüro hier?
4 Haben Sie einen Tisch? In fünfzehn Minuten?
5 Ich möchte etwas trinken.
6 Mein Urlaub in Florida war sehr gut.
7 Wo gibt es eine gute Pension?
8 Kann ich bitte die Rechnung für das Telefon haben?
9 Wir waren nur einmal in Köln.
10 Meine Kinder sind jetzt gross genug.
11 Um wieviel Uhr sind Sie morgen in der Firma?
12 Ich bin immer von halb acht bis Viertel nach fünf da.
13 Eine Frage bitte: wo sind die Toiletten, geradeaus?
14 Wir möchten im Januar nach Oslo fliegen. Aber es ist zu kalt.
15 Kostet das mehr Geld?
16 Wo sind Sie morgen um halb elf?
17 Es ist schrecklich, es gibt nicht einen Job ohne einen Computer.
18 Können wir hier jetzt essen, und haben Sie Platz (or Plätze) für sechs?

19 Wir haben ein kleines Haus in Amerika, aber es war sehr teuer.
20 Auf Wiedersehen, wir fahren jetzt nach Hamburg.

YOUR SCORE: ___ %

Week 3

Test your progress

1 Können Sie einen Verkäufer sehen?
2 Wo können wir etwas zu essen kaufen?
3 Wann müssen Sie heute in die Firma? Um sieben? Wie schrecklich!
4 Wir haben das gestern im Fernsehen gesehen.
5 Ich glaube, die Geschäfte sind jetzt offen.
6 Gibt es hier ein Kaufhaus oder ein Zentrum mit Geschäften?
7 Entschuldigen Sie, gehen Sie auch zur Post?
8 Wo haben Sie die englische Zeitung gekauft?
9 Wer möchte Wein, und wer möchte Bier trinken?
10 Das Wetter ist morgen schlecht. Das ist nicht nett.
11 Das ist alles? Das war billig.
12 Die Briefmarken kosten genau fünf Euro.
13 Der Geldautomat ist für alle Kreditkarten.
14 Sind 300 Gramm Käse zuviel? Nein, kein Problem.
15 Es gibt eine neue Reinigung drei Minuten von hier.
16 Haben Sie bitte eine Tüte für meine Schuhe?
17 Ich glaube, ich habe hier eine Apotheke gesehen.
18 Ach, du meine Güte, alle Eier und drei Flaschen sind kaputt!
19 Können Sie das sehen? Ist das Baumwolle?
20 Grösse zwölf in England – was ist das hier?

YOUR SCORE: ___ %

Week 4

Test your progress

1 Ich bin sicher, unser Termin war Dienstag.
2 Heute? Nein, das ist nicht möglich. Wir haben leider keine Zeit.
3 Ich muss ein paar Sachen für meine Freunde kaufen.
4 Können Sie mir bitte helfen? Ich möchte die Nummer vom Arzt.
5 Wissen Sie, wo es ein gutes Restaurant gibt?
6 Ich glaube die Kirche ist sehr interessant, aber niemand möchte sie sehen.

7 Wir möchten nächsten Montag abend fliegen.
8 Können Sie mir bitte die Speisekarte geben?
9 Haben Sie ihm Ihre Papiere gegeben?
10 Kann man hier Obst und Gemüse kaufen?
11 Kennen Sie sein neues Buch?
12 Es war wunderbar, vielen Dank für den netten Abend!
13 Warum müssen Sie meine Kreditkarte sehen?
14 Die zwei Wochen auf der QE II waren ein bisschen langweilig.
15 Sie sehen den Geldautomaten oben am Ausgang, bei der Tür.
16 Wir essen Huhn oder Bratwurst – der Fisch ist zu teuer.
17 Wie sagt man auf deutsch...?
18 Wissen Sie, wo es hier einen Bus gibt?
19 Mein Mann fährt gern nach Texas, aber ich fahre lieber nach Arizona.
20 Sie haben nicht gesagt, wo dieses gemütliche Restaurant war.

YOUR SCORE: ___ %

Week 5

Test your progress

1 Diese Tasche gefällt mir nicht, die andere Tasche war besser.
2 Wieviel kostet die Fahrkarte – hin und zurück.
3 Was haben Sie gesagt? Können Sie bitte langsam sprechen?
4 Ich weiss, dass Benzin in Amerika billiger ist.
5 Es ist verboten, in der U-Bahn zu rauchen.
6 Ich kann nicht warten. Ich habe einen zweiten Termin um elf Uhr.
7 Ist dieser Kasten für Briefe? Ein gelber Briefkasten?
8 Hallo, wir sind 30 km von Hannover. Ist das die Werkstatt?
9 Was ist schneller: der Zug oder das Auto auf der Autobahn?
10 Est ist diese Woche sehr heiss. Ich möchte lieber ein bisschen Regen.
11 Er hat die Ampel nicht gesehen, und jetzt sind sie beide im Krankenhaus.
12 Ich habe sie heute zweimal an der Tankstelle gesehen. Ihr Auto trinkt Benzin!
13 Wo gibt es eine Reinigung? Ich habe Öl auf meinem Armani T-Shirt.
14 Wir wohnen hinter der Hauptstrasse, genau bei / an der Bushaltestelle.
15 Wir sind bei der Polizei, weil unser Handy weg ist. / denn unser Handy ist weg.
16 Die Fahrkarten sind billiger, wenn Sie sie jetzt kaufen.

17 Ihr Auto gefällt mir. War es sehr teuer?
18 Können Sie uns bitte helfen? Wo kann man hier am / beim See essen?

YOUR SCORE: ___ %

Week 6

Test your progress

1 Ich schreibe gern Briefe, weil ich einen neuen Computer habe / denn ich habe. ...
2 Wie geht's? Was ist los? Kann ich Ihnen helfen?
3 Wieviele langweilige Leute von der Firma kommen?
4 Ich habe nicht die Nummer von ihrem Handy. Es tut mir Leid.
5 Der Schwarzwald gefällt mir. Wir hatten da letztes Jahr viel Schnee.
6 Der zweite Koffer ist im Bus. Können Sie die braune Tasche nehmen?
7 Wieviele Karten haben Sie Weihnachten geschrieben?
8 Das ist verrückt: ich glaube jemand hat mein Steak gegessen!
9 Warum haben Sie nicht telefoniert? Wir haben bis gestern gewartet.
10 Schnell! Haben Sie ein Taxi gesehen? Mein Flugzeug wartet.
11 Wissen Sie das nicht? Der Flughafen ist immer offen – Tag und Nacht.
12 Est ist wichtig, dass Sie mit Ihrem Urlaub zufrieden sind.
13 Ich habe auf einem Schiff gearbeitet und war nie seekrank.
14 Haben Sie mich in der Zeitung gesehen? ... ohne Schuhe!
15 Ihre Mutter ist sehr nett und macht wunderbaren Apfelkuchen.
16 Wohnen Sie in Deutschland in einem Haus oder in einer Wohnung?
17 Wir müssen beide arbeiten. Drei Jungen und zwei Mädchen kosten viel Geld.
18 Wir hoffen, die Werkstatt kann das reparieren.
19 Ich kenne ihn, er geht immer mit seinem Hund einkaufen.
20 Wer hat gesagt, man kann hier nicht rauchen?
21 Wir fliegen nach Dallas. Dann nehmen wir ein Auto und fahren nach Las Vegas.
22 Ich möchte mit dem Verkäufer sprechen. Er hat mir keine Rechnung gegeben.
23 Wir haben Ihren Wein getrunken, aber wir haben zwei neue Flaschen gekauft.
24 Es tut mir Leid, aber **Instant German** ist jetzt zuende.

YOUR SCORE: ___ %

Say it simply

Week 5

(Entschuldigen Sie), Sie haben mir jetzt ein Auto gegeben. Aber die Farbe ist ein bisschen kaputt. Links, hinter der Tür. Bitte können Sie kommen und es sehen und es auf mein Papier schreiben.

Week 6

Hallo / Guten Tag, ich bin Kate Walker. Ich war in Ihrem Hotel, Zimmer Nr... bis heute. Ich habe leider im Zimmer Sachen von mir, und ich bin jetzt im Flughafen. Ich möchte die Sachen bitte nach England. Das Hotel weiss, wo ich wohne. Vielen Dank.

Spot the keys

Week 6

1 It depends when you are going. Normally it takes 20 minutes. But if there is a lot of traffic and the Bleichen bridge is blocked you have to allow three quarters of an hour. You can read the price on the meter. Normally it is roughly between 30 and 35 Deutschmarks.

2 They had of course been to ...*England!*

how to use the flash cards

The **Flash cards** have been voted the best part of this course! Learning words and sentences can be tedious but with flash cards it's quick and good fun.

This is what you do:

When the **Day-by-day guide** tells you to use the cards cut them out. There are 18 **Flash words** and 10 **Flash sentences** for each week. Each card has a little number on it telling you to which week it belongs, so you won't cut out too many cards at a time or muddle them up later on.

First try to learn the words and sentences by looking at both sides. Then, when you have a rough idea, start testing yourself – that's the fun bit. Look at the English, say the German, and then check. Make a pile for the 'correct' ones, and one for the 'wrong' and 'don't know' ones. When all the cards are used up start again with the 'wrong' pile and try to whittle it down until you get all of them right. You can also play it 'backwards' by starting with the German face up.

Keep the cards in a little box or put an elastic band around them. Take them with you on the bus, the train, to the hairdresser's or the dentist's.

If you find the paper too flimsy photocopy the words and sentences onto card before cutting them up. You could also buy some plain card and stick them on or simply copy them out.

The 18 **Flash words** for each week are there to start you off. Convert the rest of the **New words** into **Flash cards**, too.

It's well worth it!

FLASH CARDS for Instant LEARNING:
DON'T LOSE THEM – USE THEM!

1 Flugzeug	1 sind
1 bin	1 nach
1 Sie	1 auch
1 aber	1 sehr
1 arbeiten	1 jetzt
1 leider	1 wie

1 are	1 aeroplane
1 to, after	1 am
1 also	1 you
1 very	1 but
1 now	1 work
1 how	1 unfortunately

1 Ihr, Ihre	1 langweilig
1 immer	1 viel
1 Urlaub	1 ohne
2 Zimmer	2 teuer
2 vielleicht	2 möchten
2 genug	2 ein bisschen

1 boring	1 your
1 much, a lot	1 always
1 without	1 holidays
2 expensive	2 room
2 would like	2 perhaps
2 a little	2 enough

2 schlecht	2 wieviel
2 nur	2 kein, keine
2 Frühstück	2 von … bis
2 fahren	2 man
2 geradeaus	2 etwas
2 schrecklich	2 Rechnung

2 how much, how many	2 bad
2 no	2 only
2 from … to	2 breakfast
2 one	2 go, drive
2 something	2 straight on
2 bill	2 terrible

3 gehen	3 müssen
3 heute	3 zu, zum, zur
3 zuerst	3 kaufen / gekauft
3 Geschäft	3 gestern
3 wann	3 sehen / gesehen
3 Verkäufer	3 wer

3 must	3 go
3 to	3 today
3 buy / bought	3 first
3 yesterday	3 shop, business
3 see / seen	3 when
3 who	3 sales assistant

3 glauben	3 später
3 Stück	3 sagen / gesagt
3 dasselbe	3 mich
4 jemand	4 warum
4 Termin	4 wichtig
4 Sache	4 möglich

3 later	3 believe
3 say / said	3 piece
3 me	3 the same
4 why	4 someone
4 important	4 appointment
4 possible	4 thing, matter

4 nächste Woche	4 ach so!
4 oben	4 wissen / gewusst
4 fertig	4 sagen / gesagt
4 ihn, ihm	4 sicher
4 natürlich	4 hinter
4 geben / gegeben	4 niemand

4 I see!	4 next week
4 know / known	4 at the top, upstairs
4 say / said	4 ready
4 sure	4 him
4 behind	4 of course
4 nobody	4 give / given

5 hin und zurück	5 Fahrkarte
5 Zug	5 sprechen / gesprochen
5 warten / gewartet	5 beide
5 nehmen / genommen	5 dass
5 weg	5 weil, denn
5 zufrieden	5 Hauptstrasse

5 ticket	5 there and back, return (ticket)
5 speak / spoken	5 train
5 both	5 wait / waited
5 that	5 take / taken
5 because	5 gone
5 main road	5 content, happy

5 Haltestelle	5 Kasten
5 Tankstelle	5 Benzin
5 Handy	5 Werkstatt
6 Leute	6 ihnen
6 Weihnachten	6 zuende
6 ihr	6 nichts

5 box	5 stop
5 petrol	5 petrol station
5 workshop, garage	5 mobile telephone
6 them	6 people
6 finished, over	6 Christmas
6 nothing	6 her

6 richtig	6 wohnen
6 sie hatte / hatten	6 sein
6 Wohnung	6 nie
6 Flughafen	6 Mutter
6 Schnee	6 Junge
6 Mädchen	6 schreiben

6 live	6 right
6 his	6 she had / had
6 never	6 apartment, flat
6 mother	6 airport
6 boy	6 snow
6 write	6 girl

Wir waren im Mai in Berlin. 1

für meine Firma 1

Entschuldigen Sie, bitte. 1

Ich arbeite bei Rover. 1

Wir haben jetzt Urlaub. 1

Sind Sie aus London? 1

Wir sind aus Manchester. 1

Ich war bei Shell. 1

Sie hat eine Freundin. 1

Wir fliegen nach Mallorca. 1

We were in Berlin in May. 1

for my firm 1

Excuse me, please. 1

I work at Rover. 1

We are now on holiday. 1

Are you from London? 1

We are from Manchester. 1

I was at Shell. 1

She has a friend. 1

We fly to Mallorca. 1

Haben Sie ein Zimmer? 2

Es ist kaputt. 2

Wieviel kostet es? 2

Von acht bis halb zehn. 2

Das ist zu teuer! 2

Wir möchten nach Berlin fahren. 2

Wir möchten etwas essen. 2

Wo gibt es hier ...? 2

Wo ist das Café? 2

Um wieviel Uhr? 2

Do you have a room? 2

It is broken. 2

How much does it cost? 2

From eight to half past nine. 2

That is too expensive! 2

We would like to go to Berlin. 2

We would like to eat something. 2

Where is there … here? 2

Where is the café? 2

At what time? 2

Wir gehen heute einkaufen. 3

Wo gibt es einen Bus? 3

Es tut mir leid. 3

Wir müssen zuerst zur Bank. 3

Ich möchte Schuhe kaufen. 3

Das ist alles. 3

Wo gibt es hier einen Supermarkt? 3

Wann sind die Geschäfte offen? 3

Wir haben viel gekauft. 3

Ich habe bei Karstadt gegessen. 3

We are going shopping today. 3

Where is there a bus? 3

I am sorry. 3

First we must (go) to the bank. 3

I would like to buy shoes. 3

That is all. 3

Where is there a supermarket here? 3

When are the shops open? 3

We bought a lot. 3

I have eaten at Karstadt. 3

4

Jemand hat telefoniert.

4

Er hat nicht gesagt, warum.

4

Ich habe einen Termin mit ihm.

4

Ich kenne ihn.

4

Das geht nicht.

4

Können Sie mir das geben?

4

Können Sie mir helfen?

4

Essen Sie gern Bratwurst?

4

Ich trinke lieber Wein.

4

Wie sagt man … auf deutsch?

Someone has phoned. 4

He did not say why. 4

I have an appointment with him. 4

I know him. 4

That's not on. 4

Can you give me that? 4

Can you help me? 4

Do you like eating Bratwurst? 4

I prefer drinking wine. 4

How do you say in German…? 4

Wo ist der Bahnhof? 5

Wann fährt der Zug? 5

Wie kommen wir zur Autobahn? 5

Wohin fährt dieser Bus? 5

Gibt es hier eine Werkstatt? 5

Wir nehmen das andere. 5

Es gefällt mir nicht. 5

Es war billig, weil es alt ist. 5

Die Tasche ist weg. 5

Ich hoffe, dass Sie ein Auto haben. 5

5

Where is the station?

5

When does the train go?

5

How do we get to the motorway?

5

Where (to) does this bus go?

5

Is there a garage here?

5

We take the other one.

5

I don't like it.

5

It was cheap because it is old.

5

The bag has gone.

5

I hope that you have a car.

Nächste Woche muss ich arbeiten. 6

Ich kann nicht warten. 6

Wo wohnen Sie? 6

Ich muss mit ihm sprechen. 6

Wir haben eine Dreizimmerwohnung. 6

Unser Urlaub ist jetzt zuende. 6

Was ist los? 6

Wir haben zwei Tage gewartet. 6

Haben Sie das gesehen? 6

Wie geht's? 6

Next week I must work. 6

I cannot wait. 6

Where do you live? 6

I must speak with him. 6

We have a three-room flat. 6

Our holiday is now over. 6

What is the matter? 6

We waited (for) two days. 6

Did you see that? 6

How is it going? / How are you? 6

InstantGerman InstantGerman InstantGerman InstantGerman

This is to certify
that

....

has successfully completed
a six week course of

Instant German

with .... results

Date *Instructor*